JOHN JORDAN

COLLECTED POEMS

EDITED, WITH PREFACE AND NOTES BY

HUGH MC FADDEN

introduction by Macdara Woods

DEDALUS

The Dedalus Press
24 The Heath, Cypress Downs, Dublin 6W, Ireland

ISBN 0 948268 85 9 paper
ISBN 0 948268 86 7 bound

The Dedalus Press receives financial assistance from
An Chomhairle Ealaíon, The Arts Council, Ireland.

Cover Design: Graphiconies

Clóchur: Peanntrónaic Teo.

PREFACE

This volume of Collected Poems brings together in chronological order of composition all of the verses of John Jordan which I have been able to trace. It consists of the poems from the four volumes published in his lifetime: – "Patrician Stations", (New Writers' Press, Dublin 1971); "A Raft from Flotsam", (Gallery Press, Dublin 1975); "Blood and Stations", (Gallery Press, Dublin 1976); and "With Whom did I Share the Crystal?", (St. Beuno's, Meath 1980, hand-printed by John and Barbara Deane); – along with the poems previously published only in magazines or newspapers, together with the verses discovered among his manuscripts at his home in Park View Avenue, Harold's Cross, Dublin.

The chronological ordering of the poems should redress the imbalance caused by their previous printing history, when they were published out of sequence in a manner which distorted the author's dialogue with the reader. Here, for the first time, is the progression of a pilgrim soul, as Mr Jordan fashions the myth of his life, from the astonishing precocity of such early works as "Pub Poem of the 40's", "Ghosts in Marble", and "Second Letter: to Patrick Swift", through to the poignant melancholy of "In the Nine Winters" (1954), and "Tidings from Breda" (1963-70); reaching a powerful maturity in the poems of *Patrician Stations*, and culminating in a rich individuation.

Mr Jordan's stature as a poet has not been fully appreciated yet – except by those peers among his contemporaries who were secure enough in the knowledge of their own talent not to feel any jealous sense of rivalry regarding Mr Jordan's undoubted abilities – writers such as Patrick Kavanagh, Austin Clarke, Pearse Hutchinson – or else by those younger poets who blossomed in the halcyon days in the Sixties when John Jordan was editing *Poetry Ireland*, when he had "the blinds up and the door on the latch".

John Jordan, in his lifetime, had his audience, his distinctive "peoples". This collection should ensure a wider readership for his work. Also, it may encourage literary critics and academics to pay proper critical attention to his verse. Even the anthologists may reconsider their arcane choices.

This volume needs no further comment from me – except to paraphrase Ezra Pound's "Note for T.S.E.", on the death of Eliot.

His was the true *Patrician* voice – not honoured enough, and deserving of more than we ever gave him. Here, I will not write of my friend, John Jordan, but will state with some urgency: Read him.

Hugh McFadden
literary executor
Dublin 24-2-1991

John Jordan, by Edward McGuire

CONTENTS

THE POEMS

INTRODUCTION

In the Summer of 1962 I visited John Jordan in the James Connolly Memorial Hospital in Blanchardstown, when he was recovering there from pulmonary tuberculosis. Resident in a grianán of Noel Browne's as he later put it, or taking a rest, as Patrick Kavanagh has it in his poem, "Literary Adventures", written at about this time:

> There are three swallows' nests in the rafters above me
> And the first clutches are already flying.
> Spread this news, tell all if you love me,
> You who knew that when sick I was never dying
> (Nae gane, nae gane, nae frae us torn
> But taking a rest like John Jordan.)

Love comes into it, as it always did where John was concerned. It was a lovely day, a fine sunny day, when I set out to visit the grianán, bearing a flat fifty-box of Players cigarettes as a gift, and when I arrived I found the patient in triumphant form, as sunny as the weather. His room was bright, there were rows of glossy, interesting-looking, review books laid out on a table beneath the window, and exotically splendid in lilac pajamas and dressing gown he looked just the man to do the job. He was in command and in control and, it appeared, enjoying himself enormously.

The afternoon passed easily in fun and chat, he served us rations of whiskey, his in a glass, mine in a tooth-mug which he first scoured ostentatiously under the hot tap with pantomime flourish and business. For, as he said, "When you get to my age you know about these things." Later a party of his friends called in on their way home from the Races, glamorous creatures quoting odds and gossip, until by the evening I had smoked more than my share of the cigarettes from the flat Players box, and ended by eating his supper. He felt it would sustain me on my journey back across Dublin, as indeed it did. And taking a rest he may well have been, after his own fashion, but as always it was a rest to some purpose.

In the Autumn of that same year the first number of the reconstituted *Poetry Ireland* appeared with John as editor, taking up from the previous *New Irish Writing/Poetry Ireland* which had been edited by David Marcus and Terence Smith, S.J.White, and Valentin Iremonger, consecutively, over the decade 1948-58. It is in the nature of small poetry magazines to be courageous, news-sheets from the barricades. This new *Poetry Ireland* was certainly courageous, and it also had intelligence and grace. Austere is a word which has often been used of John; to some extent I suspect this is another way of saying what is true, that he was never vulgar, and this was true too of *Poetry Ireland*. Its horizons were wide, its options open, and it was concernedprimarily with excellence. In the first editorial he stated the matter at its simplest:

> We are concerned with the publication of the best available verse by Irish poets or of special Irish interest, but we will attempt to include verse outside these categories, including translations. We are committed to no school, no fashion, no ideology. But we abhor mere opinion. We would wish, in the humblest of ways, to contribute towards the recreation of Dublin as a centre of letters. We hope we have the blinds up and the door on the latch.

The recreation of Dublin as a centre of letters was no small order. As I remember it there were few if any outlets for verse at this time. The only exciting publishing event that I can now recall was the single issue of the *Dolmen Miscellany*, also in 1962, which contained prose and verse by writers including John himself, Richard Murphy, Pearse Hutchinson, John Montague, Thomas Kinsella, Aidan Higgins, and others. The appearance of *Poetry Ireland*, and its continued appearances, was therefore a matter of major importance in the living culture of this island.

The blinds were indeed up, and they remained up throughout the sixties, and the light from the windows made possible the appearance of the short-lived *Arena* and the even shorter-lived *Holy Door* – both epoch-making in their way – and extended the existence of the *Dublin Magazine*. Because it created an atmosphere in which such magazines could function, and, perhaps more importantly, one in which they might be given due recognition and credit, John Jordan's publication, quite simply, formed public awareness and perception of literature in this country in its time. And since it consistently had breadth of vision and a high standard of production, the hall-marks of its benign and fastidious editor, its influence, and his, have extended far beyond the final number in 1968. It is arguable, for instance, whether *The Lace Curtain* (1969), *Cyphers* (1975), or *The*

13

Poetry Ireland Review (1981), could have come into being if there had not been that space prepared for them.

Poetry Ireland changed things, and for this alone we owe John Jordan an immeasurable debt of gratitude. But of course there is more to it. There is his own work. When he died in 1988 he had forty years of literary endeavour and achievement behind him as editor, critic, story-teller, and poet, and as academic, broadcaster and man of the Theatre. The very variety of the disciplines makes it hard to achieve a clear view of any one of them: when you focus on any one thing another stands out.

The marvellous radio talk on Aogán Ó Rathaille, for example, in the RTÉ series "The Pleasures of Gaelic Poetry," gives way to the piece on Seán Ó Ríordáin *(Cyphers* no. 12), which in turn gives way to the piece on Caitlín Maude *(Cyphers* no. 23), and how to reconcile these with the high camp of the stories about Rose MacMenamin, Jemima De Róiste, et al? And how to reconcile these in turn with the poems on Julius Henry Marx and Micheál MacLiammóir, Anna Wickham, and Mae West? Is it all waste and wilfulness in the end, disordered fragments?

For all John Jordan's sense of fun, and there is undoubtedly a wilfulness about much that he wrote, there is a common factorapparent throughout, a seriousness of purpose. The range of subjects is not finally antic, but is part of the serious record of a complex and erudite individual obsessed with the connections – the Baudelairean *correspondances* – of things. A person for whom the crack in the tea-cup opens not only onto the way to the land of the dead, but also on perilous seas; where Mabel Mercer figures at any given moment with Jacques Prévert and Judy Garland and Fred Astaire, with Pity and terror, with Phèdre, Pierce Ferriter, Jean Cocteau and Thomas Mann, with Will Hay, Denis Devlin, Teresa of Avila and Francois Villon, the theology of forgiveness, Barnes, MacCormack, and Stephen Hayes, with Love and Death, the fortitude of Islam, Nathanael West, William Barnes and Linden Lea, all of which could surface in any one night's conversation. For a veteran polymath and polyglot of the human condition, as John was, in the end it is not merely surprising that *John* MacCormack should sing *William* Barnes, least of all late at night, in Leland Bardwell's basement flat in "Low Leeson Street".

Polymath and polyglot he undoubtedly was, and with it he always reminded me of the character in Borges' "Poema Conjetural":

Al fin he discubierto
la recóndita clave de mis años...

He could never as yet quite make such a claim but in the
meantime he searched for it with courage and dedication, and
sent back poems, telegrams, and messages of recognition. He
described the poems disparagingly as verse, and called them
"Sunday Poems", but if verse they are then it is as Michael
Smith put it in the Irish Times Profile of June 14th 1988: "verse
(but) in the best sense of the word, as applied to the work of
Pope and Swift or his beloved Dr Johnson or Austin Clarke;
intelligent, controlled, erudite, witty, deviously punning,
mischievously satiric". And it was also very much alive;
compassionate, troubled, questioning, wise, and serious. He was
not, in fact, a "Sunday Poet", he was rather an occasional poet.
Again in the best sense of that phrase.

The poems are called up by, and deal formally with, events
such as births, deaths, hospitalisations, coincidences of time and
place. He wrote his poems to the occasion and for the occasion
as it arose, but always seized the opportunity to consider the
wider implications, the sometimes apparently unresolvable
implications, of being a human being and remaining a human
being, and yet, somehow, not being deluded. A deeply religious
man, a "Catholic in the European sense" who on more than one
occasion noted that Hope is hard, he also brought a tough
Protestant rigour to bear on his lifelong application to the
problems of faith and forgiveness, and in this he could, and did,
call on the traditions of Bunyan. To be a pilgrim, in this
tradition, in itself has grace, is worth the candle, and with
Bunyan he believed passionately in the necessity of seeking out
salvation.

The first collection of his poetry to appear, late in hiswriting
life, treated of the whole subject of forgiveness, and treated it in
depth. This was *Patrician Stations*, published by Michael
Smith's "New Writers' Press" in 1971. *Patrician Stations* is an
important contemporary religious poem and the "New Writers'
Press" publication was an honourable enterprise, but, ironically, I
feel that in the event it may have done John a disservice in that it
both ignored and upstaged everything that had gone before.
Publishing, at the best of times, is akin to Russian Roulette, a
potentially lethal business dependent on luck, but John's
publishing history seems even more *à rebours* that most. By
1971 he had been writing poems for some twenty-three years, his
own personal mythology was established and in place, and by

15

disregarding it he left his proposed audience, and indeed himself, without any clear terms of reference.

I can understand the desire to get the new work out, to put it before the public as soon as possible, but I believe it may have puzzled the public. The fact that a book may puzzle people is not a reason for not putting it out, but there is a particular kind of coherence to John's poetry, the recorded progression of a Self, in which the past is peculiarly important to the present. The language and landscape have been established, there are references to a lingua franca which has already been decided upon and accepted before the curtain goes up, in the case of the date of publication of *Patrician Stations* some twenty years before. The lingua franca of the book is accessible, but naturally enough, only entirely satisfactorily so to those who have read the poems that went before.

> Past is not past.
> More than the blessed air
> It pumps us into wakefulness
> Sustains ache for lilac
> Long since swept down the drains.
> "Tidings from Breda"

"Tidings from Breda" is a dark, frightening poem, which took seven years in the making, or the unravelling, and in a way it clarifies one of the anomalies in John's life at the time. Which is, that although he was "very well known as a poet" throughout his twenties and thirties, and as critic, story-teller and editor, throughout the sixties, I do not believe that all that many people had actually read his poems. These had not been collected together, and had not been widely available. It is a truism that a poet without an audience is dead, but certainly a poet with a body of work that has not been put before the public, for whatever reason, will find, sooner or later, that the work has begun to tell against them, and against itself. The kind of anger and puzzlement which can result are clear in "Tidings from Breda":

> My bestiary is for sale, my love,
> There are for you slashing reductions.
> But may I suggest that crook-necked nag:
> Give him a carrot, some hay,
> Sugar at Christmas and major feasts.
> If you have to bury him

Let it be far from the furious Swan.
If you have to skin him,
You may find a boy of ten
A-jingle with medals step-dancing
Tears to his mother's eyes.

It is a matter of some amazement to me at this distance that
when I became a student of John's in University College Dublin
in 1959 I was totally unaware of his poetry. In fact the first
poem of his that I encountered was somewhere about this time,
in an old copy of *The National Student* dated 1949: "Second
Letter to P.S." (Patrick Swift):

Mine was a mime of lime-scent and heartbreak
quiet, frail, imbecile, thirsty for applause
– and O you knew that and nurtured me, because
Thespis's children stick together
in sunlight and shower and weather
when the proud rose must surely fall,
thrown on a dump with all the rest of the trappings,

In *The National Student* that poem was dated 1948, and it
was not until 1975 that it again appeared in print, and this time in
some kind of context, in the collection of "versifications", *A Raft
From Flotsam*, published by Peter Fallon's Gallery Books. In *A
Raft From Flotsam* I find twenty pieces dating from the period
1948-1954, and among John's papers at the time of his death
there were a further eight unmistakeably so dated. It is not a
huge output for a six year period, John's entire body of poetry is
not huge, but it is respectable and one can only wonder at this
remove why there was no collection then or later.

One answer may well be fashion. The few publishers of
verse that existed in Ireland in the fifties were not all that
interested in the human heart, or at least, not in the human heart
as John Jordan celebrated it. Books of poetry did appear, but
perhaps his fastidiousness did not permit him to push to have his
work among them. He was never a Committee-Man nor a hard-
nosed operator or self-promoter, if anything he erred on the side
of appearing at his most vulnerable before those who could do
him most harm.

Whatever the reason for it, there is no question but that the
poems lost a degree of relevance by not being published in their
own context, in their own time and place, and for all his very real
humility about his "verse" it must have been a matter of

17

appalling anguish to him that his work remained to all intents and purposes invisible for more than half his writing life. And along with this there was obviously a further uninvited difficulty in trying to communicate with an audience that remained ignorant of the validity of his mythologies. It is good, but no more than time, that his work has appeared in context and in order.

The persona of the early poems, 1948-1958, is solitary and observant, reserved, almost dandified in a nineteenth century sense. Even the love poems manage to be genuinely erotic and distant at the same time:

> And I see you with care, with tenderness...
> Slowly and grave entering the sheets,
> Your careful rapture as you explore again love's valleys,
> The mysterious woods where peace should be.
> "An Old Letter", London 1951

There is a continuous thread of melancholy throughout, a tone of elegy for the lost Self, an ever-present awareness that things decay and that promise fades. Sometimes the disenchantment invests the work with a kind of suspension and paralysis, it becomes obsessive and enclosed. The Self begins to turn against the Self, distaste becomes destructive. A Pinchbeck Greco, he calls himself at Oxford, in this piece, dated 1958:

> At peace in sunlight
> Pinchbeck Greco come to rest,
> He is disfettered from his native world,
> Peaceable in gold.
>
> Never, he dreams, again
> The cool guests, the invited quarrels,
> The moons that look on no harvest.
> "Self Portrait"

The real truth is that promise fades for everyone, not just the gifted and precocious, and the fact that promise fades does not make the promise itself any less valid. What is left for the poet, and more particularly the occasional poet, is getting on with the business of separating the prose and poetry of life. And when this is working satisfactorily, as in the following, it opens up possiblities beyond mere stoicism:

18

In the nine winters of our discontent
We unflesh pity for a thorned motive
In new departures from required perfection,
Groping for succour of unsteady images
From childhood, death-bed, private blackness.
With these we sow the creepers of our giving,
Master our crabbish scuttle from taking.
"So long, God, and my Galatea
I've just noticed my heart is breaking".

So on we travel to the next shipwreck
Followed by the Fisherman's inland bird.
The creature's voluntary skewers the elegy
Sung in a fathom's knowledge of sinking,
Drowned for a hank of yellow coarse hair,
Marinated for a daub of love.
Dead lovers rise from new shipwrecks
Often and most amiably are drowned:
For their nine winters they dream the knowledge
That cock and gull make the same sound.
But Galatea and my God,
I'm presently waking.
Have you lost your senses?
My heart is breaking.
          "In the Nine Winters", Oxford 1954

For all the grave tone of most of this poem, the reserve and
austerity, the apparent aloofness even, it is not arcane or elitist.
It is not removed from the immediacy of reality. On the
contrary, the poet is dealing with hard considerations here, and
he is dealing with them in the hard words of the artisan: skewer,
hank, daub, coarse hair, sow, creepers. The abstract terms, too,
sound hard in context, "Pity" is set beside "thorned", perfection
is sharpened and pointed-up by being required, private blackness
is made more concrete by coming after childhood and death-bed,
which in turn come together in the back of the mind, child-death-
bed, child-birth, death in child-birth. It is with these concepts,
this material, that we sow the creepers of our giving, master our
crabbish scuttle from taking. Almost without noticing it we have
moved to a perspective in which the whole of human endeavour
can be stated in a couple of words. Giving and taking, getting
and spending, a time to live and a time to die. The religious
symbolism works as well as it does because it is so casually
employed. It is assumed that we will be familiar with the

19

progression flesh-thorn-succour-death-bed-giving-taking, as indeed we are. It is almost an abstract of Christian belief. Abstracted further and applied to common human experience in the second stanza, but grafted onto such messages as those of "The Winter's Tale" and "The Tempest" where storm and shipwreck are prerequisites to salvation, where images can take on life, where there is a second chance and time can be redeemed. Or can it?

> But Galatea and my God,
> I'm presently waking.
> Have you lost your senses?
> My heart is breaking.

In the nineteen sixties John began to feel that the city of Dublin was closing in on him, as a person and as a writer, for all that he was working on several fronts as critic, editor, and full-time academic. "Dirty Dublin", he called in in "The Haemorrage", his commemmoration of Gainor Crist, written in 1964, "Dirty Dublin (where) my enemies were attempting to confound me." Were it not for the necessity of earning his living, he writes, he would be tempted to stay on in the hospital in Barcelona "reading detective stories in French and dipping occasionally into harder matter, and there would be letters from the Dear Ones keeping me in touch with the mushrooming City of Dublin, the goings-on of the young poets, the peregrinations of various hearts with whom I have nothing in common but possession of a similar organ. Something similar." For all the jaunty bravadothere is a sense of real pain here, and certainly the kind of public life he chose to lead in Dublin left him unguarded, on view, and open to contumely. All small urban societies can take dissimulation in their stride, if anything it makes things easier, and in a sense John was simply too spontaneous. As I have said, he was never an operator or a self-promoter, and he never acquired the ruthless brass neck that is the mark of the invincibly, measurably, successful. But in the end he remained his own man.

"The body was found to be sane", he writes in "The Haemorrage", "God was very good to me and I am intellectually grateful. But I tasted my own blood and so I will never be the same again", That event took place over Christmas 1963, and it would be tempting if one were to judge only by the "Tidings from Breda" (1963-70) to regard the rest of the decade as a seven-year dark night. But this would be untrue. He always kept his European avenues open. As ever precocious he had hitch-hiked round Europe in his teens and it simply never occurred to him at any stage of his life to regard himself as anything but European. Any pronouncements he might make about the human heart in Ireland must hold good for Europe as well, for, as he said: "(the nursing jargon is) international, like love." And although the European option may not seem remarkable now, it was genuinely remarkable some forty-plus years ago, and for at least a decade after. The continuing reassurance of the values of European civilisation and his adherence to them, could, to some extent at least, balance the Chimeras which haunted him in his thirties: the notion of failure, and his not-quite-shadow engagements with the powers of darkness - "the snide faces with their mean tricks and their unimpassioned jealousies, and their ignorance of purification."

Certainly the late sixties was a time of great personal distress for him. I was living in London at this period and he stayed with me on a couple of occasions when he was passing through on his way to the Memorial University in Newfoundland. For several years he had been racked by ill-health and accident, and by doubts and by too much drinking, and despite the gaiety and courage and fun during these visits there was also a quality of desolation and despair about him, a reiseangst which had to do with more than travelling. In 1968/9 he paid a long visit to North Africa, visiting his friend Dr Richard Riordan in Tripoli, Libya, and later in the year he spent the first of several spells in St Patrick's Hospital, a guest of the Dean in James's Street, Dublin. Now for the restless unsettled occasional poet, writing to and for the occasion, here at last was the occasion rising up to meet the poem.

Everyman has a singular future, he wrote in "Tidings from Breda", mine is failure. To which paralysing assertion there is not very much that anyone can say, either in concurrence or denial.

Al fin me encuentro
con mi destino sudamericano

says Francisco Laprida, the hero of Borges' poem, on the point of death. Reality is often clearest out at the dangerous edge, and in no fanciful way it may well have been part, at least, of John Jordan's "destino" to write a precise and authentic, undeluded contemporary religious poem, and to write it not from a grianán or a bee-hive cell, but from and for a "madhouse". From

21

Jonathan Swift's own particular foundation at that, just to copper-fasten the matter.

Patrician Stations opens in a wide magisterial sweep, and it continues throughout with a high tone which is nonetheless never allowed to become grandiose. More successfully here than anywhere else he intersperses the high tone and high seriousness with his own throw-away references and his own particular brand of slang - an argot impossible to fit into any one chronological context. The lines are discursive and loaded with content, but they remain light and airy.

> Great Dean, invigilator of our loves and liberties,
> Here is United Ireland. The burrs of thirty-two counties
> Stick in my heart. That cool twelve thou' has
> Bought me fraternity. We are all experts here.
> Schizophrenics, depressives, alcoholics, pathics,
> Some elated like the Blessed Saints, others
> Withdrawn to who knows what red hell or
> Candid heaven, all are duly elected members,
> Acadamicians who may never resign, signatories
> Of the treatment.

The cool twelve thou' - a nod in the direction of Nathanael West, a taking aboard of Miss Lonelyhearts - has founded Ireland's first truly democratic Institution. The Eye of Heaven blazes on us all alike, the strollers in the Gardens of Welldorm, the Artane Band among the roses, the Legions of Gardenal inspecting the dahlias, and the Surmontilised clock-golfers beating the rap:

> Each soul dead-set for personal salvation.

And yet United Ireland has its constipation problems, since in the nature of Institutions regularity is all. Even the men involved in the 1969 Moon landing, then in progress, must be punctual if they are to be caught on the telly, while the life in the hospital moves inexorably on at the pace decreed by the Treatment. Tomorrow when men have landed on the Moon, our democracy will still drop marmalade, slobber porridge, let fry cool, tea tar, valued butt incinerate.

> We are all experts here. Elated and withdrawn
> Will find the Moon their common ground.
> Boozers will start out of pre-planned temptation,

The sick of Eros will goggle at heart's craters revealed,
You, great Dane, chained on your parthogenetic rock,
May remember when the Moon had its liberties,
When the Liberties had a Moon and a Man in it.
Pray for us, reluctant Prometheus. Remember
The House of which you are the Father.

While this first poem in the *Stations*, "A Guest of the Dean's", has an hallucinatory drugged atmosphere, the second poem, "The Feast of St Justin", is clear and sharp. There is a feeling of having moved on from one psychological state to another, or from one part of the hospital - or from one stage of treatment - to another. There is a new sensory awareness, references to this chillier air, that spiky air, that chill at the feathers. Removed to another part of the Baudelairean "forest of symbols":

Ego ceases to self-canonize, play Everyman,
Florentine, those creatures that gibe or whatever
In William Blake.

And while there is a proud spaciousness, a "magnanimity", about urbane wit and wisdom, civilised discourse, "sapient chunter over Montaigne", magnanimity is too easy while forgiveness - like Hope - is hard. Forgiveness is not only concerned with the monsters, the mass-murderers and the torturers, the offenders against the Holy Ghost, but also with the minutiae of human life. A son's brusquerie to his mother, as well as dethroned eyeballs, skewered genitals. And who will judge the norms of guilt:

Will Picasso be forgiven for his pretty white dove?
Will no account be taken of Iscariot's love?

And what about the Staff, Medici Sancti Patricii, who take away the patient's clothes, will they be forgiven for refusing the Host, get a look-in when the Hosannas are vaunted?

I suppose like the rest they'll be forgiven:
Hitler and Picasso, Dali and Franco,
Frank Ryan and Stephen Hayes: the lot.

But two denials of forgiveness, one general and the other arising from deep personal hurt, put the writer himself beyond it:

23

I will not be part of the inordinate forgiveness
Since I cannot forgive the pride of thickness
Nor Newman's gentleman adjusting the batteries.

In the end there is a resolution, subtle and not altogether satisfactory, the recognition of forgiveness as a theological mystery as Faith is: we must accept the vast unreason of forgiveness; and:

Sit down to barbecue with the Johnsons and yacht-
Yickety-yacht with Onassis: there's limit to exclusiveness.

And we may pray that acceptance, the grace inherent in themystery of forgiveness, will itself redeem forgiveness. Will lend a recognizable sense and meaning to it.

If this resolution does not seem immediately satisfactory, it is nonetheless true to its context, it is true to the spirit of the sequence, and it advances it. The next section, "Letter To Paul," addressed to Paul Durcan and his wife Nessa on the occasion of the birth of their daughter, is essentially a celebration, an incantation of blessings on that event. There is also another change in perspective on the part of the writer. He has identified the figures in his landscape and has separated them. Self has now become selves, the thousand and one selves of a self scissored from its native motley. As before, all humanity is there, including the beast, but now at this juncture magnanimity is appropriate in the offering of cradle-gifts, in the celebration and benediction of a child. The child is the closing of the sacred Delta:

Man, woman, child are Trinity,
Semen, blood, milk, a binding mixture.

And all human experience is acceptable and proper in this context. May she be "At the right time herself a Conceiver/Of Trinities, in her own right a Blessed Person." And this includes the possibility of heartbreak and loss:

Even nightingales heard in Berkeley Square
Are not to be sniffed at, if she's a woman
At all: she will be the better for human love,
But like drink, not too much of it.

24

The last of the *Stations* in the version from the New Writers' Press - a fifth poem "A Paella for Drivellers," was added to the version which appeared from Gallery Books, in 1976 -is "Heimweh", Homesickness. The "Letter to Paul" is sent specifically from "my chambers in James's Street", the recluse in the hermitage is magnanimous but he remains a recluse. "Heimweh" on the other hand is concerned with the world of the "infrequent 16A and the price of vegetables." This emergence/resurrection, it appears, produces a feeling of "homesickness", which must be suspect in a world where hospitals, prisons, and drastic therapy, are the manifestations and machinery of the normal. To have Heimweh for a madhouse is, at least, "invidious". To love fiercely the faces of the violently unhappy:

> Minds with just that one mote in them,
> The thread that coarsens the turnip:
> Such love is certifiable, the lover a fink.

But then, Christ too was a fink, a freak, a freak who went in for love-feasts, suffered the "ministrations of tarts". His Father

> Put him through most drastic therapy.

At a time like that, resurrectionary thoughts were not, I'd say, a balsam.
And the idea occurs that all the collective motes of the minds of all the violently unhappy:

> might make a beam
> That would sustain a sane world, my masters,
> And utilise Spandau for preventive purposes.

Who'd be sent there and by whom is matter for another poem.

"A Paella for Drivellers", the next poem in the sequence, goes some of the way towards answering that. There is always another circle of hell below the one in which we find ourselves, and if our hell is tolerable we feel it can't be real. Pain, like truth, must be absolute. The ostensible occasion of this poem is a reported incident in Limerick when Robert Graves refused to enter the White House pub until a photograph of Ezra Pound which was on display there had been taken down. This story enables John, who loathed sanctimoniousness and cant, to set

25

himself in St. Elizabeth's alongside Pound, almost in fact, as it were, as well as in spirit. St. Elizabeth's is properly his place, not this Swiftian haven where even the mad are human; he too should be in St. Elizabeth's because his heroes are people he fears to fight for:

> Jews, Sephardic and Ashkenazy,
> Palestine refugees, disloyal Kurds,
> The world's great galazy of Nansens,
> God's chosen miserable.

And because he demands miracles, and is at the same time terrified of life and of God, and of himself. This last poem is more uneven than the preceding ones, but there is a street toughness to it, however fragmented, which was not present before. Rather than expressing an intellectual nostalgia for vaguely Villonesque characters, he seems here to be recognising and itemising the genuine article. And the psychological tension is also right, the stance of a gambler who has played an unusual version of Pascal's *jeu de pari*, and lost the toss. I am afraid, and:

> Lord, I am grateful even for being afraid,
> And I remember you Faith Burton
> Who thought you were a tram.
> And you dear Covington who were bled by faggotry, Gesinus
>   and leukemia,
> And Anton of the grimed ivory neck...

The itemisation becomes in turn a litany and a prayer, and ends in absolution:

> Above all, Lord, Unknown God,
> I am grateful for finding
> My choate tiles of splendour
> In poor human beasts,
> Not in *putti* or medallions.
> These human things are all we have
> God. Unknown, or *à la* Nine Fridays
> Be good to them. God bless *le moineau*
> And make her a good girl.
> Rich and rare were the gems she wore.
> Now we are rid of our greatest carbuncle.

I have already mentioned how I feel that the publication of the *Patrician Stations* in 1971 may ironically have done a disservice to the work which went before. To consider the *Stations* in isolation would be to extend that disservice to the work as a whole. They are to do with some unfinished business, the settling of some personal spiritual matters. This does not make them any less valid as a public statement, because they do put matter upon a number of things which up to then had been unclothed mnemonics. But they are not an end to anything, not even the end of a movement. At the time he was writing the *Stations,* John was also investigating other parallel directions for himself in verse. As before, the time out was devoted to a regathering and redeployment of forces.

In *A Raft From Flotsam* (1975) there are four poems dated 1969. One of these, written in Tripoli, Libya, obviously predates the *Stations* by some months, but the others are contemporaneous. There are another six poems in the same collection which date from the early seventies, and a further thirteen poems from the seventies in *With Whom did I share The Crystal?* (1980). There are eight more, identifiably from this period, and there are a further three which were published in magazines, two in *Cyphers* 19 and 25, and one in the 1983 issue of Hayden Murphy's *Broadsheet.* And there were plans. On the cover of *A Raft From Flotsam,* he wrote: "I note with mild interest, that from my thirteen years as a practising academic, the only pieces that have survived were written outside Ireland, where I hope to pass the remainder of my days in comparative torment." As it turned out, fourteen of the poems post-dating that note were also written outside Ireland, mainly during various sojourns in Spain.

The pattern of his life might appear to have been taking on a familiar, even a classic turn, and in a sense it was. But in the same way that he always distanced himself from what he called The Hound of Heaven Stakes, it would be wrong to consider him as any kind of latter-day Sebastian Melmoth. He was, in fact, highly regarded in his own country as a man of letters, and was a Member of Aosdána, for example, from its inception in 1980. He was held in high esteem by his peers as a meticulous and penetrating critic. Time and again publishers mooted plans to gather at least some of the critical pieces together, only to have the plans fall through at the daunting size of the task, the sheer volume of work involved. A collection of short stories, *Yarns,* appeared from the Poolbeg Press in 1977. He continued writing stories over the next decade, and was hoping to put a second collection together at the time of his death. And yet the fact remains that he was not widely published in book form during his life, and there is no entirely satisfactory explanation for it.

The truth is that he did not fit into any category, nor, more often than not, do his poems. Although the later poems in particular are, at their best, perfect examples of unhurried, unforced, apercus, balancing compassion and intelligence, a civilised man's considered statement to the moment. And, again at their best, there is a marvellous free-wheeling toughness and apparent looseness to them, which enables him to speak to the point on his heterogeneous variety of subject matter. Saints, Film Stars, Politicians, Suburban Gardens, Dope Peddlers, Love, Age, Dignity, the present Pope, and Groucho's sophisticated Marxist point of view. The tone is light and spacious, zany even, but it does not derogate from an awareness of pain and frailty: St. Joseph of Copertino, in an ecstasy of enthusiasm:

> seized the Confessor of
> The Convent of Fossombrone,
> Took him, men, on a trip.
>
> But O the Chevalier Baldassare
> Who had fierce O such fierce tremors!
> At Assisi they say it happened.
> Joseph grabbed him by the hair
> Wheeled him round in aether
> And from the brightness of the air
> Set him down safe O untrembling.
> > "Flying Men" 1979

Whether "sloshing through the cafe-au-lait pools" on the lane between Doohat and Annaghmakerrig, a journey I remember making with him in 1982, and considering a native-born Monaghan peacock on the way, or sitting among the blazing azaleas of the Parque del Campo Grande and deciding on the true message of Groucho Marx: Let the people have duck soup:

> Chiefly, let them raise intemperate eyebrows
> To the infinite spaces of the stars.
> > "For Julius Henry Marx" 1977

the voice and utterance are consistent. It is the voice of a man who will not consider the fearsome Staff Nurse, Irma the Terrible, whose scorn would frigidate the Bold Fenian Men,

28

without also considering "that Albanian nun who rescues little ones/From garbage". Who, when writing of the illness of Dolores Ibarruri also remembers:

> Kathleen Daly Clarke
> Whom we exported to English welfare,
> And her spouse the tobacconist.
>> "During the Illness of Dolores Ibarruri" 1977

There is a cord of genuine human sentiment strung through all these connections. And in three poems in particular, the elegy for Micheál MacLiammóir (Málaga 1978), the poem for Kate O'Brien, (Valladolid 1977) and the poem for Gerald Brennan (published in *Cyphers* in 1986), the occasion, the moment of poem and statement, and the sentiment, are caught and fixed together, almost as in a Cartier-Bresson photograph. The result is unsentimental and heartstopping: "Doffed the curious toupees /Unflaked the valorous *maquillage*:"

> The great player relaxes
> (Does he smoke a Celtique?)
> Waits for this ultimate call.
> O what will people say?
>
> In a sub-tropical garden
> Drenched in moonlight
> Moths, midges, white butterflies,
> Die on my cheeks,
> As I cry for you.
>> "Micheál" 1978

The infinite range of the possibilities of meaning and simultaneous meaninglessness of the silences behind words is caught in the statement of the Manager of the Hotel Jardin, in Avila:

> When I told him you were dead
>> (Dead, though you walk beside
>> me, cloaked, ribald, vulnerable)
> His dark mild eyes crinkled,
> The argent real was in his threnody:
> *La pobre Mees Katie* – twice
>> "Without Her Cloak" 1977

29

The old, the frail, the sick, have as much right as any of us to take risks, to fall, to injure themselves, to be wrong, to die, in their own fashion. On the fourteenth of May, 1984, Gerald Brennan, at the age of ninety, was brought from his home in Alhaurin el Grande, Málaga, to a home for the old in Pinner, Middlesex. On the twenty-first of June he was brought back to his house in Spain. The sad, pathetic story, has something heroic and epical about it, something that is closer to tears than to words. Something fragile and grand:

> I wished to die, but yes, I wished to die,
> till they said I'd drive them mad,
> but not in a clean and well-lit place,
> exiled from my things
> from my black tobacco,
> from my roses,
> from the street
> Carlos Gross had them name for me,
> poor Carlos whom I've survived.

> *Quiero morirme*
> here in Alhaurin el Grande
> Babbling they'd have me believe
> of my dear glamorous shades
> of Lytton and Ralph and Carrington,
> of Leonard, Virginia and Morgan,
> yes, I wish to die.

> Only let me connect,
> dreaming, dreaming, dreaming,
> till they raise the coverlet
> beyond my nostrils.

And now it is done. I have tried to add a few notes to the record of the passing of a very singular man, and I have done it – I hope, with love. It occurs to me that I may have erred on the side of darkness and given too little room to the love and laughter that always surrounded him, and if I have I am sorry. He was, quite simply, one of the most loveable people I have ever known. Those who knew him well will need no reminding, those who did not will have to take it on faith. Though not entirely on faith, there are, after all, the poems, the hundreds of thousands of words of literary journalism, the critical pieces, the short stories, the radio broadcasts, the writings of those whom he was the first to edit, encourage, and publish. There are the erstwhile students – the first wave of whom must now be over fifty. There are the literary magazines dotted matter-of-factly about the country, and the small presses turning out a healthy sum of books each year, and a greater public understanding of the place of literature in our lives. All in all, it is a better scene than that which confronted him as a young writer in the fifties, and the improvements are due in no small part to him.

Macdara Woods
Dublin, Jan 1991

TWO LOVES: 1

Her hair was burnished,
her eyes sombre with puzzlement,
her voice a sad birdy twitter.
The puppets ringed about the pond:
and, God, the pain of finite words,
the rounded agony of footling speech.

1947

ADOLESCENT

Standing naked like a thin parsnip
Desire on his shoulders pressing him down.
Old saws heard in chalky class-rooms
Prickled his head like a thorny crown.

Curled pyjamaed in Jack Frost sheets
Blossoms at his loins dying from drought
Evil lessons learnt at ash-spumed tables
Curdled his heart with fear of being caught,

Crushed between the pages of the dusty yellow novel
Currently read by the old and the queer,
Love expelled till tomb-time to webby corners,
Palping and stroking, the mind never clear.

Can lust be banished by God's gratis luxuries,
Art, the sunset, swans, the history of the moon?
Will love ever come with his clean white linen,
Cover the shame of the sad naked loon?

1948

ON A FRIEND IN LOVE

They'll not forgive him,
Because he has not learnt the cosy tricks,
Like faked horse-sense,
That lure the comfortable, the advising, the middle-aged.

They'll never understand
That even in the oddest places,
Sootherin' Filda in the Abbey Bar
Stretched in Baggot Street – nothing can mar
His vision of the many-peaked star
That shines for men of art.

Part of what he tells us is utter nonsense
Part of what he tells us he does not mean
Part of what he tells us, tells to the perceptive
Why his eyes are like the sea and green.

But still we fear
That the too frequent tear,
And the hopeless thrall of a Yankee flapper,
May blast the vision, darken the eyes,
Pack off art with sophistry and lies,
And we shall raise a keen in the Abbey Bar
For the single-mindedness nothing could mar
"O he broke his teeth on a hard old stone
He loved like a pearl of the sea".

All join in and raise your glasses
'Gainst golden lads bound to brazen lasses,
"O he broke his teeth on a hard old stone
He loved like a pearl of the sea".

10th July 1948

SHEPHERD'S WARNING

Help me shake off this shroud of envy
Stifling worsted that chafes the brain,
Let me be content with sun-rise ever scarlet,
Drabness of sun-down, threat of sharp rain.

Let me no-more long for the sun-sets of others
Nor wince because they have known the dove.
Graft in me patience, will my sunsets scarlet:
After the deluge shall come my love.

1948-1949

KATIE

For Katie the candle-glitter and the pine are worth the frost
At Mass-time in the Winter.
The household lie till nine until sausages and scramble
When already she has knelt and clacked
A thousand Aves – Mary's marvellous currency
Of worn sweet words –
Earliest of payments for Katie's feather-bed
When the candles sputter out in the lambent night.
Bread of angels for breakfast when she goes home
Back beyond the womb and the scalding light.

1948-1949

FIRST LETTER: To Donal O'Farrell

Do you remember?
We share one basket and I dip to find
Me a schoolboy, primfaced, soft, refined,
Some said sexless, some said unkind,
Mouth twisted by a hymn to gods I didn't know about.
Did you? odd goblin friend, wan as a straw
Craning your neck like a swan in the straw,
– Reeds in the canal in the sun are like straw –
Opening your mouth to say "maw" instead of "more"
– Did you?

Do you remember the sun atoming the dust
Of green, of blue maps, of salmon-pink squares,
The white mixed grill of Hall and Knight,
Chill, chaste Euclid, that swan who ticked off Ptolemy?
Do you remember our great blind mother
And her servant crows who beaded eyes
On us canaries in her leaky chalk-fumed cage?
Our first silk-light knowledge of *lacrimae*,
Virgil born by the long green fat canal?
Your elucidation of my heart's eccentric page?

Of course we'd have been better
Playing manly games,
"Knicks, knicks, football-boots and jerseys",
To have known the frenzy of boot and ball
Like all the forgotten lads who
Yelped above at their pigeon in the placid grey,
The unknown lads whose old men's memories
Will kindle the damp sod,
Mud-caked knickers and dungy boots,
Their brothers' hortations at the end of day.
And I think of you now and
Find me a schoolboy – have you forgotten,
And will you still forget,
Like the swan in the straw
(Reeds in the canal in the sun are like straw)
But no more.

Dublin 1948

37

NOTES FOR AN OBSCENE SEQUENCE

The silver fox, my darling,
Will gobble up your breast,
O strip yourself, come quick with me,
Be naked, that's the test.

Our trees of iron are just as fine
As shoots of flowering shrubs,
The martinis of my kisses
As good as gin in pubs.

You'll soon forget the pleasure-trips
To Mayo or Shanghai,
But in the end you'll always feel
My hand upon your thigh.

So throw away the chicken-legs,
Come fasten on my mouth,
And when you're glutted there, my bird,
We'll take a trip down South.

Dublin 1948

PUB POEM OF THE '40s

1

"Come, come, come!"
    Cry the Men of God,
And why in God's name don't I go?
But other mummers die
And the doxies they cry,
There are more things in life,
Than brass tacks and a wife.

"Come, *do* come!"
    Cry the Painted Men,
But why in God's name don't I go?
For me that mummer died,
For me his mother cried:
There are worse sides to death
Than rouge and baited breath.

The solution might be
To make a pass
At a decent, healthy,
Catholic lass,
With desirable papa
And intriguing thighs
And imbecility in her eyes.

To settle down (but where?)
Outside the town's the thing
And you'll always sing
If you're early to bed
And late to rise – and
What a simply smashing surprise,
When on a cold dark winter's night
She coyly whispers that the prize
Of strictly modest copulation
Is a Blessed Event – ah what elation!
For we shall have done our duty!
And as everyone knows
(Including that priest with the mottled nose,
That charming thing who gave me a rose,
The boy who at Seapoint was chary

39

The Scouts and Gampdom of Sairey)
Duty is beauty!

2

But rarely, perhaps, to go alone,
Alone on days with mist
When the glass moon comes early
And unseen gulls skim phantom
Barks that bear across the darkish water
My dear unreasonable courtesans.
Their milk is gamey
Smacking of fried fish and future pain.
They travel far with easy hearts,
And forget with whom they've lain.

Into the train!
Home to the daughter of J.J.Quinn
Home to the love that's free from sin,
And the Pope has sent us his blessing!
(Conveyed by the Bishop of Nara)

"Pray for the Pope's intentions"
"The Fires of Hell" said Father Molloy
While in the front row squinting at a boy,
Sat Kate who is a modest dove
Well-grounded in the perils that attend Free Love,
But not as nice as Peggy P.,
Who in one's green days used to be
A good-time girl with risky males
And quite a dab at dubious tales:
In fact she held the bed quite dear,
But finished up with a skipping queer.
"Three Hail Marys for the Conversion of Russia".

3

There was thin blue light
Where some stars had upstaged
The clouding glass moon.
It annexed partially from the night

40

A fairly classic head, blonde hair,
A nape ending in shadows.

The rain had spiked us
Bone had gone to marrow-fat,
Eye to eye had grown unlike,
There were new hard pebbles in love's pockets.

The wind had towelled us,
Back to bone went attainable flesh
Limb grew to limb again familiar.
Lovers whisper their assuring axioms
Forget that the weather can catch them out,
Bodies come together as perfect strangers,
Terrified, mysterious, until the death in doubt.

4

Wake my love no more in nightmare,
Devil-goats should not be near,
When inside my arms I hold you,
Unless it is myself you fear.
Fear perhaps may be contagious,
Even when creatures are at peace:
Sometimes, child, I fear to lose you,
Since flesh, being weak, must beg release.

5

Flesh calls to flesh across the ramparts
Built by some spirit to protect its love,
But an aureate head may spin a halo
Persuading flesh that spirit has removed,
Tenanted another fleshy habitation
Where for a new death we're on probation.
Since each loss erases past possession,
We find that love has missed the bus,
And solitary, since we left the womb,
Romance up the night as personal doom.
There is some hope for little Peggy P.
But God of Love, is there any hope for me?

The Painted Men grow old,
Cold invades the veins
Where the blood of strangers pulses.
Clay triumphs over alchemy,
Brimstone guts the dressing-table.

But their plumes still wave
Above the screaming trees,
Wave their signal of unending love.
The glass moon, their complacent madame
Smiles, so tender, on their follies,
The stars shine for them
A macula especially.

But don't forget to pray for the Pope's Intentions,
Every single Sunday the P.P. mentions
Nuns, priests, abroad are very badly pressed
Bringing God to black babies and ensuring they're dressed.
Yes, pray too for the destruction of the Reds,
For all poor occupants of unchaste beds,
For disgraceful dipsos, sods, and tarts
Joyces, Gides, and Jean-Paul Sartres.

And may Christ have mercy on us all.

Dublin 1948

ODE TO MICHAEL GILL, ESQ.

1.

O to have a little still
To set up house with Mickie Gill,
Porter always on the table
More spirits than we would be able
To drink, beneath the kitchen stair
And in the cellars brandies rare
Liqueurs the best were ever sold
Sherry for the luscious gals of old
Who knew us when in cold and rain
We yearned to have the precious bane
When all we had was "plain" and rhyme
To while away the limping time,
The darkling days when ne'er a client
In all of Dublin could we find.

2.

O how we'd savour rum and gin
And brandy cocktails that'd win
A prize at any high-class do
From Portobello to Peru.
To see the starlight shine on whiskey
And greet the tricky moon as frisky
As lambs that gambol on the green
And after if for more we're keen
O then there's bottles rowed on high
To help us clutch the velvet sky!
And then to bed to dream of more
And no wolf howling at the door
Nor fear to face the coming day
For well we know what you will say
When eyes are thick and heads are chronic,
"Why don't you have a gin and tonic!"

Dublin, 1948

43

WORDSWORTH WAS RIGHT

"At eight-thirty a.m.
A Titian-headed girl
Said good-bye to her mother
Going down the steps
Through yellow light and the trees
Away to the beaches and May".

"That's beautiful". And the way she says it,
Her eyes all warmth, you'd think
She surely meant it.
What's the purpose of the lie.
What's the purpose of the great room,
Where the trailing cobweb glistens
And the ghosts tap their bones on the piano-lid,
Shuffle the sheets of Debussy, and the dust
Settling...
Do you know what I mean?

What too's the purpose of training American glory
Under subtle pretence of business and the like...
Yet was that glory sweeter than the violets
Wet, wet violets sold in Stephen's Green,
Gentler, sharper, sharper than the candle-flame,
Candle guttering in Pembroke Road.

Listen people...
Only he could tell us the truth about it all:
The man who worried epic out of the sod
Stamped on the ashes till they glowed
The man who gleaned the lyric at the heart of the clod
The man who reaped what he sowed.
But how well we know, yes, what he would say,
Crashing through the cobwebs (lovely cobwebs!) to the
           fine raw day.
Listen people...
"That's not poetry! Pure shite,
                    pure shite!"

"Yes, Patrick. That's very well put. But
Don't you think..."
"The Muse is queer. She's like a goad.

44

Poetry's never written unless a man's
All on fire to do it, on fire with
Happi-
        ness, on fire with
Sor-
        row".

O to get out of it
O to get out of it
O to get out of it
Or drink the Shannon dry!

Ah the eyes are warm again and the May days
Have come back to the room.
Crackling paper, spilling water,
Beautiful shades out of business.
Ah the eyes are warm again,
"Read us another one John".

"At four-thirty a.m.
A white-haired woman
Said good-bye to guests
Leading them down the steps
Through the night-stock fragrance
Out into the reaches of November".

Dublin 1948

WORDS AND MUSIC

Have you ever seen a roomful of black people dancing?
The grace and glee of it. More grace indeed
                        than in white gulls gliding
From green water in the Green.
And sad strength. Twisting, yearning,
                        crying the youth of soul
Flying in plumages of wonder-days.
All the small canaries sang in our hearts,
Chirruped in awe at the counterpane jesters.

The canaries sang
The day after,
The day after that,
And part even of another day.

Dublin 1948

GHOSTS IN MARBLE

A worldly beauty by the world forgotten.
White gardens, golden domes and domes
      scaled green and blue like a fish
And cypress and steps and cupids in gold and white plaster,
      and garlands and groves of flowers,
Live doves and doves of clay that fly over the blue trains
And a marble head of Massenet and the sea laughing below:
Even the mountains think that you are dead.

I dreamed when I was a boy
That you were dead already, that the soul had died in you
      long ago;
And the girl at my side had the same dream.
You were a bauble, a griffin, a white armadillo
We said, and we looked at each other's eyes and laughed.

That first night long ago
Long ago.
You were a plaything we said, a mad doll, a white
      wedding cake
Of honey and sugar and sugar plums and a heart
Of marble in your breast and a little tune
By Massenet you played
As you lay among roses in a gilded trellised box:
A casket of false gold alone in empty silken space
Painted to represent the sky. O well; it may be
We were right as we sat there – how young we were –
On azure straw chairs on a terrace
Under the dazzling umbrellas.

The world that lay at your feet
Was a world of flies:
Flies forever feasting off your sugar-marble flesh
So meticulously painted
And the sun and the moon shining down on you.

Maybe that first night we were right
And you were a gaudy fantasy of princes and of merchants.
But one day, suddenly, we fell in love with you
Desperately and bitterly as one can only fall in love
With negligence, with bright and wanton indifference.

And tonight I am looking at you out of the eyes
            of that old sterile love.
Tonight you are the loneliest thing in the world
And now you dream from dawn until night comes
And dream again and stir most pitifully
Under your sleep
And the flies no longer hover round you
To gnaw your heart away, and I think
That you are more bravely decked now than you ever were
In your bright past (beauty you never had)
More bravely decked, more elegant, more leonine,
Your flowers, your gloves, your jewels
Your painted eyes gold-lidded watching the sea forever.

******

The wheels still circle in your heart
Those polished glittering wheels that brought you fame and gold
But you no longer think of them, you are indiffreren
To wheels and fame and gold alike
You have forgotten them as a man in his strength
Forgets his heart and all its traps and snares.
No, you dream of gold no more: your dream tonight
Is of small distant figures
That rise and fall, draw near and then recoil,
Your dream tonight is of dancers. You
Who have a myriad tongues
Are dreaming tonight in the tongue
Of Russia, in the language
Of dancers.

Dance again, imperial dancers.
Although the stage is empty, the lights all dark
Dance. Here is level holy ground
Dance once again.
Your dreams are dense with ghosts:
Diaghilev walked on this ground long, long ago
The young Nijinsky by his side, docile, inexorable,
(Was it the Fool, grown divine, leading a King
Into the stormy dark?) And after
Nijinsky, Massine:
Meticulous, matriculative, limitless: then

48

Dolin came: the lonely slow-shot arrow of elegance
Passing leisurely out of the bow:
And Bakst, Picasso, Braque, Stravinsky,
Karsavina, Spessitseva, Nikitina, Danilova – queens
Diamond-eyed, snow-sandalled, swift-flying
Among the shadows of other shadows
Of friends and lovers who are dead
ANd who walk here for ever
Walk under starlight and the straight beams of the sun
Here in immaculate gardens on moon-blanched marble
And others still who whisper and laugh and talk
Of painting, of philosophy, of dancers
Forever young, because they are dead.

Oh you, my heart's love, you and I together
In loneliness of spirit in the loneliness of the gardens
We look at each other suddenly and laugh
And I remember that first night and that first laughter
Long ago
And the girl who is dead.
"A wedding-cake, no more..."
O, forsaken beauty by the world forgotten,
O, elegant heart-breaking solitude,
Forgive the words: for how
Could we have understood you at the first swift
                              breathless glance?
How could we have known?

It is quiet here: a white-footed silence
Steals past us like a sigh. I think that I could stay
                              here forever with you,
And all of us, we three, I and you and this white place,
Remembering that ancient laughter, that faintly mocking echo.
But suddenly you say "I cannot bear it
This dead and dreaming
Elegance, this ghost-filled moon-drenched
Worldliness: these are your ghosts, not mine,
Your ghosts, not mine..."
                              And desire fills me
And fills these gardens
To share our ghosts with you as I would share
All things with you
But my tongue lies like a stone,
I turn my eyes away and stare

49

Across the sea to where the moon
Cuts a bright road for her feet so light
Upon the water,
And I am glad that life is as it is
Although you think this place a tomb
As the mountains themselves have thought.

Only this place and I know this:
They are mistaken: the mountains are mistaken,
To dream of dancers underneath the moon
Is to eat of honey sweeter far
And more powerful far than death.

Monte Carlo 1948

SECOND LETTER: To Patrick Swift

Dear P.,
    This letter may explain better
    than words of the mouth,
    words, words, words,
    that soothed our drought
    through rain and stars,
    the mockery of dawn,
    we cold as the trees.

For you must keep in mind
that we are less than kin,
but more than kind, for

    While you were ranting your lyceum lines
    careering the vaults of your glittering dooms,
    bleeding at the heart from paper knives
    I have my nuances and Chekovian glooms –
    But we were both mummers, and so we got on.

    Mine was a mime of lime-scent and heart-break
    quiet, frail, imbecile, thirsty for applause
    – and O you knew that and nurtured me, because –
    Thespis's children stick together
    in sunlight and shower and weather
    when the proud rose must surely fall,
    thrown on a dump with all the rest of the trappings,

        the split gold tights
        the ragged brocade gown
        the mothy ermine choker
        the sweet tinsel crown

    and our cascades of pasten jewels,
    bright as tears,
    worthless as tears,
    your tears,
    my tears.

    Yes, mine was a mime of lime-scent and quiet heart
    yours one of cypresses, and blood on the snow
    but we both were mummers and didn't care to know,

51

to realize,
to dig,
to pick away the paint,
to clutch the hand lovingly
around the white skull.
Skull last seen in the dead of night
or glimpsed at waking in the submarine light,
skull precious ivory,
to be kissed and touched tenderly...

As you may have noticed
the games are done
and I for one, my friend, am very tired.
I must confess, too, I find it hard
not to have regrets,
for years spent in plays
so unworthy of our talents.

    It will be difficult to adapt ourselves to
    ordinary life. And of course we'll always be
    peculiar, rearing the head, pouting the
    lips, stancing the body, when a stranger
    comes into the room. You know that as well
    as I do.
        Yours,
        John Jordan.

Dublin 1948

A SEDUCTION OF THE '40s

She was a fine girl, amber, supple,
He was a real fine boy, long-lashed.
She said to him one night
   (When they were ending a chat
    About Pico – him with the Golden Hair)
She said to him one night:
"Come up, come see me one night"
The trouble was they both had brains.
So he went up to see her one night.
She had a very nice flat
With lamp-shades designed special
And a photo signed *le gach dea-ghuí*
By an Irish actor, and rows and rows of books.

There was a balcony too and they looked down into the garden
And he said, "You know, darling,
Your breasts, I mean bosom, is like apples".
She said "Don't give me that crap".
They'd both seen Bogey in *Casablanca*.

She was a great girl and they had six gins with orange.
She said, "I do think you've got a tiny waist for a man".
So it went on to 2a.m.
He stood up, took off his jacket,
Went to the window and said,
   "Let us walk out where people look out
    On trees and flowers and wonderful affairs,
    And never look in on death and sin,
    Excrement of the unspeakable mind,
    Insolent bully"
Or words to that effect.
And she said "Gee".
He sat down beside her, put his hand on her bosom.
It opened out to him
Not at all like pippins.
She said, "You'll have to leave".
So it went on to 3a.m.
He stood up, took off his shirt.
Dixit: Now that the sleeping time is come
And love's musk scents the air
Let us lie down and cease to wear

Our bottoms out in foolish talk,
Masochistic jabbing.
Dixit: I don't like the use of that word "bottom".
Dixit: It's about time we
Learnt that the heart's no pincushion.

And then, you know, he put out the light,
And they went to bed and were unhappy everafter.

Dublin 1948-49

ECLECTIC

Sweet Sacrament
Divine transmutation
Flesh into spirit.

Rubble of garments
Unwashed teacups
Gibbering danger
à la Graham Greene

(Thomas McGreevy
Thirty years ago
Gnashed his Catholic teeth
At our bitch of a world)

(Thomas McGreevy
O'er the Bank of Ireland
Heard unearthly music
Passing westwards)

"What are those yellow...?"
"Oh they're chrysanthemums",
The music began
In a phalanx of flowers.

We went west
At two in the morning.
We came back at five
And the music died.

Sweet Sacrament
Divine transmutation
Spirit into flesh.

1948-49

"MY FRIENDS, MY GUESTS, MY COMRADES"

My friends, my guests, my comrades,
Come to a party – O
what a party -
My fine fornicators, my gallant grotesques:
There will be skulls to drink from,
and rose-strewn beds of pressed chocolate clay.
Where lovers all night may torment the limb and heart,
my queens, my captains, my soldiers of Christ.

And Death herself will be my hostess,
my joy, my sky-woman, my sister of mercy:
Her bleary eyes like mountainy pools,
Her sagging lips, Her fabulous infirmary perfume:
My love, my blossom girl, my heavenly music.

And there will be a floor-show – O
what a floor-show -
Six syphilitic-saddened pansies will sigh and samba.

1948-49

56

RUGS

Rugs scarlet and purple, lemon and orange,
smooth to the skin, though not meant to be worn
next the skin,
rough hairs at the fringes, though, to acerbate the skin.
Rugs, lemon and scarlet, purple and orange.

Four persons went to be a rug.

    A Hungarian man
    An Irish man
    An English woman
    A French woman
    (but of the latter I'm not certain).

The Hungarian was amused to toast-warmth:
his amusement was the kind that presupposes
a ring of birds about his head and a jug of
beer at his belly –
little fat chuckle-tablets slid from his gold throat;
the throat had become a perfectly-working slot,
through respect for the foolishness of the French wife
who indeed, though she stroked and palped the rugs
did it with polished passionless fish bones
and was damnably hard to satisfy.

And then (O my dear!) the English lady
- she was bored to marvellous whoops of laughter
beautiful lunatic *récherché* of past rugs bought
of feet the sadder by a good thirty years
sloshing through the reaches of green and red snow:

And the Irish man – he being raw from an operation on the heart
-wished he might be wrapped in a rug
lemon or purple, scarlet or orange,
and left to blaspheme or say "Hail Marys".

Ten days have passed since the fairy waved
her wand, the bitch,
turning my rich white wedding-cake
to a wafer of water-biscuit.
Something of the kind must have
happened to that Irish man.

London, Sept '49

TWO LOVES: 2

Horror it is to think of pride:
to realize, if I had had my way
this nettled ditch that now her mind seems,
because she is grown scornful and cold,
instead would have been a meadow
skyed with blue and gold.

1949

TRAHISON DES CLERCS
for Pearse Hutchinson

Some people that you know,
An old woman peeved by defeat,
A sex-meshed codger
Whose heart does not go,
A subtle sunshine boy, one sleepy eye on
                              "every main chance",
Have abused you, all three in a row.
And I because of a secret low allegiance
To a six-hour day, a cushioned chair,
Enough cash to be able to save,
Have been silent.

Dublin 1949

A DIALOGUE
for Justin Keating

A: If wicked men came
    Down the aisle through oaken benches,
    Eager to rip the golden vestments,
    To desecrate the Body,
    Crumble the wafers with wax and petals,
    What would you do?
    Would you stand up for the Son of God?
    Would you let that boy's blood out
    On the clattering marble,
    Be beaten with gun-butts or convenient rods?
    Would you cheer up the Liberators?

B: Perhaps you'd be happy with your darling
    In the great white cities,
    Clean and smooth, poplar-lined.
    In the nights of ordered passion
    You'd beget children for whom lice
    Are creatures like the dinosaur.

    Could you face it?

C: I will too. Hack this mind
    Into biddability.
    Hear no more the whinge
    Of faith's Samsonite children.
    Walk steadily ahead, eyeless for
    The blue grotto and green pasture
    Projected by the Credos.
    I will go.

Dublin 1949

59

AN IMAGINARY BIOGRAPHY

1

He loved much in his youth
Drank deeply from the wine
Vendible tepid summer evenings,
Those Georgian days in Kildare Street.

But at fifty,
His sisters nibbled their veils,
Splashed in their sherry,
Let crumbs of Marie biscuits
Drop, cling, in the red flannel
They wore for their chests.
Frail, merry, unaware of hell,
They were full of requests
That he'd take a wife, so
Keep the stock alive, for
They had married one and all,
Grown grey mice, and small,
Known only the rind of motherhood:
Julia, Sally and Rose
Bought cousins' babies clothes,
And dandled changelings
At their player breasts.
On the whole they were distraite
And after thirty years
Had grown somewhat tired
Of watching their helpmates
Eat, sleep, shave,
Hearing them guffaw,
Drunkenly weep, of
Lying by blocks of lard,
Cold, dry, hard,
Cold as their seed.

2

Year by year they went,
Julia, Sally and Rose,
With crocuses and happy rain,

A minimum of mourning,
An excess of whiskey, and
    Their husbands said they'd loved them.
But still he was single:
Happy but for a thin pain
That caught him in the small
Of his back – that was all.

He took to gin and frolics,
He read enormous tomes,
For he was a scholarly man,
Knew Greek, dreamed of Japan.
They all said, "He is failing".
How could he have health
Scooping tinned salmon in a stuffy room?
He would wear his heart out on drink,
Die on the road without a priest
To speed him to the brink
Of plum-blossom land where *Iosagán* is so pretty.

They were wrong.
Dying he heard the hot song
Of thrushes from the Sisters' garden.
In a warm lavender room
With window blinds called fawn,
A flowery chamber-pot and every dawn
The loony chime of a landing-clock,
He dreamed the journey of his days
Glancing out at all the ways
He'd met with beauty:
Shriven, he saw beneath the skin
Of those he'd loved and lusted,
Could not quite consider sin
Moments when he'd trusted,
Staked his immortal soul
On an eyelash flicker,
Rose to glory on the pediment of despair.

One dawn that spring, plum-blossom invaded his room,
The crazy clock shrilled through the percolated gloom,
And then onwards his peace was quite extraordinary.

Dublin 1950

HOMAGE TO THE PSEUDO-JANSENIUS

The faithful, quite rightly, will not listen to reason.
From the hubris of innocence they know
The path to be as narrow as the gate.
They forsake all forms of richness
Since wavering for creatures
Most certainly entails being late,
Breaking and entering the preserves of the elect,
The pinched, fearful of fantasy,
Disdainful of cakes and ale,
The true passengers.

All the rest of it is maculate:
Clerical quip and liberal mind,
Perspectives of eternity which we're told
Art can find -
Christian Plato, the stretching by fly boys of Thomas the Ox.

The rub lies with the distant honeys,
Sienese cheek-bones, Buonarotti hips,
Challenge the Rock of Ages,
Damned by tenderness, we turn asterisked pages,
Will never, though, live, adore, be luminous
Out of this world and time.

Dublin 1950

NON DICAM

The decision has been made: I shall not tell you.
Fear, toilet-trained now, has spliced my tongue.
Fear of same debâcle as other loves' recitals,
Nasty and brutish the Leviathan of disdain.

As things are at least the knoledge,
The presence of a friable decision,
Feathery images of sesamatic words
Make tolerable a yen for sweet permission.

But dear thing must I attend
A quarantine of a lustrum
Because the hound pounces on to its desire?
Can nothing in my bearing
Key you to the cypher,
Pull out the bloody plug before there's fire?

But the decision has been taken
Resolve must not be shaken
By casual affection in your tones.
I must feed in isolation
Prune ramblers of elation
Snip all Aves and Vales
And breast-buds when I see you all alone.

Vingt ans après
In clockish time some sixty hours,
Tongue has jerked the splice,
Has opened pain.
The decision has been broken
Though to you I have not spoken.
The mines are flooded, Christ,
It's dark again.
I must build a raft from flotsam,
The vomit in the belly
Time may clear away,
Mens insana too, will perhaps be sane.
I sight already wrack, suitably inadequate,
I'll work it out in shanties,
And brave again skin-diving in the main.

Vingt ans après
In clockish time some sixty hours,
I have found coral, amber, excrement,
Armour for another soft or squally day.
For which I am truly thankful,
And can hail you, o my dear.
Salve.

Dublin 1950

GERARD DEAD 1

They told him at school about Voltaire,
How the Jesuits made much of him,
And the bright boy
Died a most horrible death.

Missioners from the pulpit warned him of pride,
Which might imperil his deathless soul,
Worse, worse than Tophet, the joy
Of choiring God be withheld.

Brothers, missionaries, a Russian salad of clerics,
Drove home His Bones and His Bloody Side,
His child-days were enlightened by baroque images
Of how gruesomely his Saviour Christ had died.

The 'orrible and disgusting details of His Death
Did not mark him nor the pathos of His Birth.
The game was worth no candles,
Candles to his gentle mother,
Heaven if anywhere lay, in bread and wine of earth.
But some candle near the heart was real,
Lit Gethsemane, lit Calvary,
Led him to kneel.

Dublin 1950

LOVE POEM
"...ma douce Permission"
Apollinaire

The sky stilettoed by the hooked branch I've seen
For the first time and silver sea-shell patterns on the roof,
The chubby crocus in the cocoa clay:
O love, one further proof.

The real arrived, grief's bunting trails along the wind,
The ruffian birds that wake me no more pain:
Love's yahoo, I will paint with them the whole world rose,
O love, my gentle proof, if it remain?

Then soon with my new sight we'll walk the powdered ways
To the inn where the peacocks pierce the summer days,
Where the air all weightless gold will beat upon our cheeks.
And time will seem the substance that the dreamer seeks.

Dublin, Spring/Summer 1951

AN OLD LETTER

To begin with and in a manner of speaking
We live in the trenches.
You are on leave in the sunlight.
Your wine glitters because it seems unending
And is unending, the heart at peace being cretinous,
Careless as child in cinema darkness.
                    I say "Careless"
But knowing you, knowing
The craters that lie before you even beneath
Crisp waters when you drift amber,
Darkness that snuffs scarlet green and golden rockets
I should say "Careful".
And I see you with care, with tenderness,
Swallowing the ruby on diapered terraces
Slowly and grave entering the sheets,
Your careful rapture as you explore again love's valleys,
The mysterious woods where peace should be.

But yet you are on leave in the temporary sunlight,
I cannot expect you, but do with all my heart,
To figure the oil and the dirt, the pus-smells,
Our bloody dreams, not of the temporary sunlight
Nor the deathless ruby, nor love's valleys
Nor mysterious woods where peace should be,
But wood-glow and tea-cups, door against the rain,
The wind noises, the dependable window-panes.
I want you to know how we wake
To the stench of tears, bloody sweat,
Eyes, heels, sore from the narrow patrols,
Lips smarted from incautionary kisses.

Perhaps that's taking it to the fair,
For we are not really in the trenches.
How you'll smile when I tell you:
No oil, no blood, no uncommon dirt here
But gradated greenery
And tranquil at the top of the garden
A green cushion, an orange chair,
A woman, a man, a boy, like you in the sunlight
But screened by pied lilac.
To end with and in a manner of speaking
I love you and we live in the trenches.   London 1951

67

THE CHIME
for B.G.Achong

Talking is as bad as not talking.
Silence is as perilous as speech.
Between the chinks of speech
Falls the hail of silence.

Telling is as bad as not telling.
Confession posits standards,
Fouls up the wells of grief,
Each glance turns hazardous.

Vision is as bad as fancy.
Certain waiting as hard on the heart
As a squinting vigil with a clock.

Say then there's no difference
Between good-will and good-bye.
Quote deep sea and devil.
Say then there's no difference.
But the difference is music,
A class of chime,
Heard at all times, at all places.

Dublin 1951

GERARD DEAD 2

1

Words, lint on wound, unwritten dedications,
Surrogate feeling, cramp in the night.
Still the true misery exists, burgeons,
The glittering ache of more fortunate
Lovers, mothers, authentic brothers:
Words dislocate local necessary pain.

2

Take those tulips festering in the death-room,
Crucial blossoms they celebrate the episode well-played,
This wood where we mourn the face we have made:
This is no dead boy but a Trojan shade,
At very least an infant from castellated Spain.

3

Words will not redeem our poor marionette,
The toy horse, wicker shoes, mauve light
Where Dietrich inspects, all plumes and ermine,
The mended linen where they have you lain.

4

The facts could not be a plain dead boy,
Who crooned in gutters with marbles in his fist,
Who perchance with innocence worked out a tryst,
Kept it through dog-days of beckoning hell,
Hurled Satchmo back at the passing bell.

5

But o brother mine your false
Brother begs that you
Intercede, plead, give the info'
On what happened.
Beg salt for my eyes,
Gripe for my bowels.

London-Oxford, June 1951-November 1953

SONG

Gone are my goblin and his fairy queen
To the shimmering city where I should have been
Had a hobgoblin not fed upon my heart
Gobbled all up a very big part,
Left me to cry on an English green,
In the shimmering city where I should have been.

London, July 9, 1951

YOUR MOUTH

I was thirsty
and I found the wine cup
and I drank from it
and now I am lonely for
that old craving.

I was hungry
and I found the bread of life
and I ate of it
and now I am lonely for
that old emptiness.

I was lonely
and I found your mouth
and I kissed it
and I am lonely now only for
death.

Dublin 1953

FOURTH LETTER: To David Posner

Dear D.,

     Because with you
Big Daddy, Justice, booms again,
Because with you the harvest of flails
Seeded by we little ones that confuse Cross and Tree,
Is again believable: I write to you.

You have known, I believe, the queasiness of Mass-time,
The temptation of solitude in the afternoon,
Nostalgia for unexplored elm-dark gardens,
That comes in with the First of Sacred June,
"The starveling is fed on Sunday mornings,
The sacred mops up the leaky profane",
Yet *grand siècle* maxims, airs from Poulenc,
Shoot across the fresh interior rain.
You who would "like to be forsaken
By tears that do not count"
Are right to have none of me
For whom the heart-strings are apron-strings,
Each romantic picnic a return
To summerdays, white lilac,
Sand-castles that, lackaday, seemed durable.

But don't bother your noddle,
I've long since mastered the role of *Désolé*,
(I've been quite a flop as *Désiré*),
I've learned from repertory the way to handle
Needless prompts from Will Hay.
Still because with you, that old bags, Mercy,
Sets up her stall in the High,
Cherubim and Seraphim
Are again believable: I write to you.
Believe me, that alone is why.

Oxford 1953

THE LANCE

Being of human kind
The spear in His Side
Brought nearer than in the strolling years
The uplifted foolish faces,
The jostling and wine-bibbing,
The touch of hot earth on His flesh,
The olive-oil and sweat smells of His people.
Perhaps with the purple flowed love
For the fig tree he blasphemed.

Oxford 1954

IN THE NINE WINTERS

In the nine winters of our discontent
We unflesh pity for a thorned motive
In new departures from required perfection,
Groping for succour of unsteady images
From childhood, death-bed, private blackness.
With these we sow the creepers of our giving,
Master our crabbish scuttle from taking.
"So long, God, and my Galatea
I've just noticed my heart is breaking".

So on we travel to the next shipwreck
Followed by the Fisherman's inland bird.
The creature's voluntary skewers the elegy
Sung in a fathom's knowledge of sinking,
Drowned for a hand of yellow coarse hair,
Marinated for a daub of love.
Dead lovers rise from new shipwrecks
Often and most amiably are drowned:
For their nine winters they dream the knowledge
That cock and gull make the same sound.
But Galatea and my God,
I'm presently waking.
Have you lost your senses?
My heart is breaking.

Oxford 1954

"ENTRE CHAT ET LOUP"

for Quentin Stevenson

Cry no more with cat and wolf
Roam no more about the gulf
Where the gallant go to dive
And being dead come back alive.

Send away the hearthside cat
Starve the wolf that did not bite.
Dive deep down for what you lack
Being alone you may come back.

Leave the twilight while you may
Find the day beyond the day
All that light that sharpens form,
Beats the wild thing back to norm.

Death is where they cannot give:
You must ask for grace to love
Far away from cat or wolf,
Dive quite alone into the gulf.

Oxford 1954

SELF PORTRAIT: Oxford

At peace in sunlight
Pinchbeck Greco come to rest,
He is disfettered from his native world,
Peaceable in gold.

Never, he dreams, again
The cool guests, the invited quarrels,
The moons that look on no harvest.

August 1958

75

ONE WHO WAS NOT INVITED TO THE OPENING OF
THE JOYCE TOWER COMPLAINS BITTERLY

They came:
Jesuits, judges, Telefís jokers,
Visiting firemen, Cork pipe-smokers,
Monumental patrons, U.C.D. wives:
Time, O you beast you, despite your worst forgives.

They goggled:
Columnists, socialites, jolly old pals,
Round the clock drinkers, Trinity gals,
Play okay-ers, the Minister, *haute couturières*:
Time, O you *pup* you, has made you one of theirs.

They guzzled:
Doctors, lawyers, departmental bosses,
B.B.C. balladmen, drawn by lucky horses,
Socialists, capitalists, Fianna and Fine:
Time, O you *fiend* you, has put you back in line.

They went:
Piling into taxis, limousines and growlers,
Titivating tipsily the afternoon's howlers:

"God it must have cost
Scott a lot of lolly.
Tell me now boys,
Does he leave the key with Dolly?"

But O you man you
It was different in 'twenty-two
When few but Cons were pro
And most of the rest were anti.

Blanchardstown 1962

76

ELEGIAC NOTES ON R.C.

1

Robert has made an exhibition of himself.
He has passed over to the decent people,
Struck a bargain with the blessed,
And the beasts in Leeson Street are mourning:
Several fellows incontinently grieved
And a couple of women who knew the truth.
O Robert among the saints
Give us your paradiction.

2

The morning before Robert's exhibition
A woman looked down, not at Kinsella's
     "Baggot Street Deserta"
But on a wide tawny desert
Where there is no Gaulle but only simplicities:
A woman washing
Beyond the lintels.

TIDINGS FROM BREDA

1.

Sweating in my underclothes in Breda,
False Greco face mosquito-swollen,
A couple of thoughts laid a
Hand on me: indecent assault
On soul.

2.

One man said, kindly Machiavel:
"Others have done what you have done,
Squandered talents, gone in for fun,
Outgrown wild oats, made a success.
In so many words, "Get out of the mess".
Spoken very wisely, not very well.

3.

Wisdom smokes from the unstaked.
Good direction is morsed from the blinkered.
But mind you, I'm inclined
To think that an earlier season
Might have found me more receptive
When *couilles* and caul were of sturdier kind.

4.

Everyman has a singular future.
Mine is failure. I'd better admit it.
It may suit you, wise men and bright girls
To wish on me flecks of glory.
But I am I. Alone I know
The facts. Jordan's Book of Records
Would shake you. My locks are gory.

5.

Barren, barren, barren:
The cicadas sing.
I've done my best these days to forget:
Lent my razor to Joaquín
(O the fruiting fig trees outside my window)
Discussed aesthetics with María Antonia,
High above the City of the Virgin:
I brought lost loved ones gossip and whiskey,
She crescented with child,
He waxed proud, bronzed, mythical,
Drunk Free Cubas with *La Barba*,
Heard, told tales of Señora Nati,
Was dropped at Prici's by Toni and Mati,
("You are too tall?," said Mati,
"You must rest more", said Nati)
At four o'clock the roosters wake me.

6.

Some good may come of this:
High above the City of the Virgin
La Barba Catalanized
The least favoured cygnet of
The Swan of Coolgreany.
An omen: light flickers,
Failure of power. Unlike that Swan
I'm slow at the go. Yet
Though he cackle at my mewling
I will not shy from his crackling.
Swans, one's told, have songs.
Pavlova bit the dust.

7.

I have been cruel for twenty years
(Or nearly), douched desires
Of undesired, homely, mad, thick,
Pot rejecting kettle:
That club-footed Yank I unhearted
That breastless girl who

79

On a go-cart
Pushed her brats across Europe
Plucked lemons for snotty faces
Plunged the stallions of madness
Through immemorial groves,
Who locked up, did not die,
Came back along the lemon track.
I would straighten, Club Foot,
I would breast you, little Carter.

8.

I descend to vermouth and dominos.
To-night the rain thrashes indoors
Chronic viewers who forget to drink
The fig trees are desolate.
Supper is late.
Catalan, ten years in Brazil
(Where the nuts come from)
Tells of Irish friend Wilson,
Higgins, Campbell, who hated the English.
Do I?
"The past is the past".
Deny self. Liberal lies are bonny.
Heart whispers,
"What a whopper, honey".
Past is not past.
More than the blessed air
It pumps into us wakefulness
Sustains ache for lilac
Long since swept down the drains.

9.

Mother Church carries her burnt babies
Reclaimed drunk suckles delerium
Happy daddy pats his joyful solitaires
Nobel prizeman serves in trance *disjecta membra*
The fruiting fig trees croon their Master's Curse.
How could it be otherwise?

10.

Sprung from credulous loins
I'm partial to miracles.
It is not beyond the cards
(The smell of dung invades)
Fifty may find me cock
Stock and barrel successful,
Wife, kiddies, house, coins,
Many visible garlands about me.
But I say my future is failure.
Late in the night of
April Eight
Nineteen Hundred
Sixty Three
I saw it.
(Master of the Short Line, forgive me.)

11.

Harden, Leland, John and Con,
Dickie, Paddy dear, Dara and the Swan,
Were among those who assisted at the Wake.
Take it pet from me, that was it
No resurrection or *natividad*.
O love it was truly all very sad.
(O Nati you should have been there!)
No rebudding of spent branches
No messages of hope for the peoples
Only jaded *collage* of my pat tricks
(Pardon treey bridge, swallowy garage)
And perhaps for Carroll's Special some stories:
Death at the Bridge of the Ball
By Juan Christi.

12.

Lights out. "Franco, Franco!"
On Mont-Seny thunder fee-fa-fums,
Mongrels, pied, black, do their David.
Rain fifes, thrums and drums:
Good Lord the peace of failure.

Calm brow, cool throat, bathed limbs,
Season for the lamb, a complex beast
When you've known paper lions:
My bestiary is for sale, my love,
There are for you slashing reductions.
But may I suggest that crook-necked nag:
Give him a carrot, some hay,
Sugar at Christmas and major feasts.
If you have to bury him
Let it be far from the furious Swan.
If you have to skin him,
You may find a boy of ten
A-jingle with medals step-dancing
Tears to his mother's eyes.
(She was a school-teacher before her marriage -
This was her youngest). But
Perhaps an old nag's heart
Can take no engraving.

13.

Toni has come with a stranger.
Cointreau has the texture of dew.
Toni's eyes are smudged purple.
I pay the bill and through the moted air
We descend to the City of the Virgin.

Breda, Cataluña 1963 - Dublin 1970

EXCORIATIONS ON MONT-SENY...

Cocks crow all day on Mont-Seny:
What fowlish pleasure, what inexpressive pain?

White, blue, butterflies,
Pastel leaves,
Light on low water
Lassoing rock.

Broken cartwheels I have seen in Ireland.
But blackberries here are small and bitter.

Guardia Civil rinses mouth with soda water.
Unlike mate leaves rifle at the wall.

Rusted white church
Looks over cock
Butterfly blackberry
Water cartwheel
Guardia Civil rock
Me
O why the rifle?

Breda 1963

ATHENS

Girls and boys from Antipodes
And west of the Appalachians
I desiderate your vigour, your all-seeing eye,
No more, no less, than your chimera.
Daunted by Acropolis
Promethean by daylight
Faraday'd in nightlight
i sit in the Square, redundant,
And read *Felix Holt*.

August 1965

TO THE PEOPLE OF LIBYA

You, who have suffered much from strangers,
Who have known the assault of many empires
Roman, Byzantine, Turk, Italian, English, American,
Still preserve gentleness, a kind of love,
And true Islamic patience,
I thank my God, your God, that I am with you.

Tripoli, 8 December 1968

IMAGIST POEM IN ISLAM

Haj Riordan
riding out of Mecca
will conquer Islam,
and MISE ÉIRE
like Lawrence's Bey.

He has just sent out for the butcher.

Tripoli, 13 December 1968

A MINOR COMPLICATION

High above the city of the Three Cities
The memories coalesce. Mustapha
Fiddler with electricity, stealer of bottles,
Donor of cabbages. Post-midnight knocks.
Rocks hurled by children the Prophet
Suffered to come unto Him. Hassan,
Camel meat, but was he truly *marocain*?
Suliman, bearer of wine and olives,
Incarnation of Islamic mischance,
His friend Bakush whose memories
Regrettably embrace the *palais de danse*,
Not least the Neighbour with his methedrine,
That other ruffian and his Jacqueline.

Never again the trek to Armando's
Never again at six in the morning
The call to prayer for arid Christian buffs
Never again this afternoon of tolerable peace
When the world is governed by doves.
No vulture can take this from me.

Detail the objects on the desk.
Twenty years ago I saw that Venus,
("There she is", said Liam Ó Briain)
Seventeen years ago that Copenhagen nude,
("Get her, dear", said someone rude)
Ash-trays, the clutter of work,
An orange, Desmond's "Artemis", lean
Script that may survive the Vandals.
A match-box from Malta, *A Lonely Voice*,
All the mystery of Islam. I am too old to alter.

We do not eat *Chateaubriand*
We discuss the man.
Pushing forty in North Africa
One drops names like Goethe,
Goes on to discuss the gloomy Dane
How Rousseau might have poured into him
The desire to confess:
"Those who mess with God are not officers nor gentlemen".
Which brings me to a pose.

Being a minor complication a friend's life is trying,
God's minor complications happen when we are dying.

But screw the doggerel.
In the middle of the journey
I see no dark wood
Only unchanging laurels
Torrents of doves
Hurtling against the wind.

Philoctetes will be my guide
I will wear my pus like alabaster.

Tripoli, Libya 1969

FOREWARNED

1.

Do you think we should measure
quality of life by prestige of stimuli?
"The power of cheap music,
'Noël, Noël'?"
Ought we anatomize if salt
Is spilt over Parma violet memories,
The seed tremor with bifurcated yen?

"Better give thanks for all feeling,
Tear in the eye for Mother Machree
Loin-shudder for lost napes
Surrogate plastic when there's no filigree."

2.

Sex they tell us is not lust
Angelic matrons tell the lost
One-night passion turns to dust:
Sex is not a handled thigh,
Holy fathers fence the gash.
I look you in the candid eye:
Sweet Jesus, if the love-lech takes me.

3.

And it did: and heart now croaks
And ravens and round my thigh
There's a scelus of ragwort.
My pillow is often wet
My tongue licks the pustules
Of squandered kisses: stains of passion
Unseen to strangers blur my pupils.
All we can hope for now is
The Removal of the Remains.

Dublin 1969

A GUEST OF THE DEAN'S
for Austin Clarke

1.

Great Dean, invigilator of our loves and liberties,
Here is United Ireland. The burrs of thirty-two counties
Stick in my heart. That cool twelve thou' has
Bought me fraternity. We are all experts here.
Schizophrenics, depressives, alcoholics, pathics,
Some elated like the Blessed Saints, others
Withdrawn to who knows what red hell or
Candid heaven, all are duly elected members,
Academicians who may never resign, signatories
Of the treatment.
 Woe to the formulators of empty oaths.
They may know again the quality of shipwreck,
Watch with eyes like piss-holes in the snow
Manannán betray his tasty kinship with Moloch,
Be trapped at Calais by the mad Irishwoman
Who thinks she lives among niggers: sniggers
Should be the rhyme. Madness is no laughing
Matter. Though some here laugh like madmen.
 In remote farms tongueless bachelors
Stash barley and juniper against demonic thirst.
Forget their caches and drive mad through
St. Patrick's snakeless night. The sheebeen is
Mother's arms. The paps are horny
With plenty. The cocks crow. Swollen
Teats are dumb. Last night their
Master was "fierce lonely".
 "Have you a drinking problem?"
"Well, I suppose, like the other lads." Your
Toms, Dicks and Harrys are here, great Dean.
You gave your lolly to found our first democratic
Institution. Paudeen and Algernon rub minds.

2.

Some who have gone from soft to hard
Have been warned by Nurse against lonely pathic.
The Eye of Heaven blazes on the strollers

in the Gardens of *Welldorm:* did the bats
Come in middle of night? The cats tie themselves
To your body? The scimitars castrate you?
The *Artane* Band parades among the roses.
The Legion of *Gardenal* inspects the dahlias.
(Great Dean, your people, yours and mine, call them day-lias).
Surmontilised, the clock-golfers beat the rap.
Cuchullains, tight-pantsed, hand the ball,
Mini-skirted Deirdres ply the racquet.
They do not pray for you at Mass, great Dane,
As your people called you.
      When the Host is raised
They think not of your Liberties or Loves,
Each soul dead-set for personal salvation
Accepts as natural bounty your crazed wish,
Forgets the torment in the ears and heart,
Would surely damn a man with two women.
      Our democracy has its fascists.
The love of man and man is "dirt". Among the
Roses and the dahlias as the all-seeing Eye
Blinks alight I'm told it's "worse than besti-itis".
(A notable coinage from the County of Laois.)
      At Courtown on holiday
Ex-inmates meet. Do they discuss
Heights of *Valium,* Scrolls of *Librium* or
Those strolls in the Gardens of *Welldorm?*

3.

United Ireland has its constipation problems.
Immemorial castor oil still has its uses.
Some of our citizens like Martin, Francois, yourself
                  great Dane,
Make us privy to their cloacal mysteries.
Bowels without compassion confuse thought,
Spanner the works: pique, bad temper!
      All the rage is regularity.
The men on the Moon must be punctual.
Many will bay if poet's image is violated
While *Welldorm* or *Doriden* is in the saddle.
Insomniacs, inviolate to patent sleep, will
Bless their sickness if they catch the telly
While others dream of Bacchus' sloppy lips,

Ganymede's slim-fit hips, Venus' abounding bosom.
      To-morrow our democracy
Will drop marmalade, slobber porridge,
Leg fry cool, tea tar, valued butt incinerate.
We are all experts here. Elated and withdrawn
Will find the Moon their common ground.
Boozers will start out of pre-planned temptation,
The sick of Eros will goggle at heart's craters revealed.
You, great Dane, chained on your parthogenetic rock,
May remember when the Moon had its liberties,
When the Liberties had a Moon and a Man in it.
Pray for us, reluctant Prometheus. Remember
The House of which you are Father.

Dublin 1969

THE FEAST OF ST. JUSTIN

1.

Removed to another part of the forest of symbols
(Latin me that, me trinity scholard)
Iveagh's cornucopia no longer rich to hand,
In fine chilled air I see Wellington gone amber
And mind skirls with aislings of Pakenhams base and blessed
And primary that Passionist Thomas one.
My thoughts are pious. In stricter air,
In perfectly unviolate insomnia,
Ego ceases to self-canonize, play Everyman,
Florentine, those creatures that gibe or whatever
In William Blake. Wellington's egg-shell now.
Match-box at stake.

2.

There's a fine fling to the term magnanimity,
The open-palmed gest, the butter of gold,
Old wine, sapient chunter over Montaigne,
I yet in this chillier air see more virtue in forgiveness,
Wonder at its almighty gradations.
Christ asking Dad to forgive Gentile and Jew;
This is immediately graspable, fist in the pale
Of ponderables, despotic and heraldic fact.
But Mary forgiving Jesus for his brusquerie,
This, my children, is of the minutiae of daily experience.
I will not understand that eighth dolour of hers
Unless there be primal mystery in forgiveness.

3.

Once
From a grianán of Noel Browne's
I saw an orange bird
And blessed the gaudy paraclete
That chose to pass my window.
Apollonian rapers have no power
Over minds saddened by maddered flesh,

Dethroned eyeballs, skewered genitals,
The minutiae, my children, of daily experience.
Will these have their part in the inordinate forgiveness?
Will Picasso be forgiven for his pretty white dove?
Will no account be taken of Iscariot's love?

4.

Peace of mind is greatest treasure.
That Passionist Thomas one, hollowed and hallowed, was
    allowed
The gluttony of blessings. Spirit can be rapacious.
But to have one's unpaid clothes secreted,
Not to be permitted that spiky air, that chill at the feathers,
Is indignity, gross though mandatory, loonish if regular.
Religio Medici is a queer text. *Religio medicorum*
Sancti Patricii best known to themselves.
Will they be forgiven for refusing the Host?
Will they get a glim of the Seraphim,
A look-in when the Hosannas are vaunted?
Facit indignatio versum: but I have no spleen against them.

5.

I suppose like the rest they'll be forgiven:
Hitler and Picasso, Dali and Franco,
Frank Ryan and Stephen Hayes: the lot.
Including the Butcher whose fleerings
Will be part of my punishment. Leering
Torturers are part of my daymares.
He'll stump around the American circuits,
Not know he's a non-figure, a cypher,
And darkling in my bosom loom to gay madness.
I will not be part of the inordinate forgiveness
Since i cannot forgive the pride of thickness
Nor Newman's gentleman adjusting the batteries.

6.

Forgive us this day
Our daily bread

92

Our ration of rice
Our peck of spice
Wrapped up in *The News of the World*.
All humanity's there including the beast.
God will be good to the pure and troglodyte,
God will be guardian to the plain and erudite.
God will be grand to us all if we accept
The vast unreason of forgiveness.
And let's face it, dears, that means we must all
Sit down to barbecue with the Johnsons and yacht-
Yickety-yacht with Onassis: there's a limit to exclusiveness.
O, I pray though, that some primal mystery in forgiveness
May redeem it. Have mercy, O Lord, on forgiveness.

Dublin 1969

LETTER TO PAUL

1.

Baptised by St. John of God,
Faith severely tested at Belmont
Tutored at Westminster on London's old sod,
Delivered, pre-packaged, to the Moated Grange,
None of this can have been pleasant.
Did you maybe turn a page here
Where Iveagh's vats dottle the thick of Summer
And their black nectar (also their harpy cousins)
Are seen only in electric box or silly-billy mirage?
      Or were you here in Winter
When the vivid casques were silvered
The pear-tree nude and unashamed
When gravel squelched and P.T. was
Always indoors, graceless concertina ballet?
No, none of this can have been pleasant.

2.

But in nineteen hundred and sixty seven
Barely zoned, you took to an untormented sea,
No longer alone, made-over by Eros' liturgy,
Coarse salt for your tongue, for your loins opal foam.
Others, purblind lepidopterists, holes in their nets,
Pursued phantom moths over almond sands,
Trekked icing-sugar wastes, were tardily sprung
By the Great Hunter (one gets tired of that Hound).
He whom they call the non-day devil
Others Asmodeus, caught us over the barrel,
Our current accounts dry, tax-gatherers converging,
Our credit dinged, our public images, dear me, quite blotched.

3.

I should speak only for my thousand and one selves,
For a self scissored from its native motley,
Life-caul sold for coils of old rope,
Imprints, signatures, conjectured dates, intaglios

On lacquer, sub-structure weeviled,
Castors squeaky: scholarship old Pollux.
For a self stripped of its supernatural drag,
Taste of wafer seasonal like rheum,
Whiff of incense in my city's streets, unscheduled prayer,
"God keep me safe, Mother Mary this night
Don't let it happen, let there be light."
For self, ah no, "selves" period: fast glaziered
When diamonds had broken and entered,
Nineteen or nine lives I.O.U.'d *in saecula*,
Splintered trusts, squatters' wrongs,
Wings of a buff flapping a dowdy empyrean

4.

Hateful ego: this is for you
And the fairy woman and the child
Called for the bride of Axel.
Man, woman, child, are Trinity,
Semen, blood, milk, a binding mixture.
I'd like to think your perhaps unattractive scrap
(A week before death Borstal Boy described
His new-born as a sausage: he was brandied)
At the right time herself a Conceiver
Of Trinities, in her own right a Blessed Person.
To that end, but not necessarily so:
May she have teeth that are neat but discreet,
May she have limbs engaging but fleet,
May she have eyes fathomless but kind,
May she have flesh that will stay unlined,
May her heart never over-step the mark,
 - Do I mean that? no, let her know the lark
In the clear air of her first mornings,
Even nightingales heard in Berkeley Square
Are not to be sniffed at, if she's a woman
At all: she will be the better for human love,
But like drink, not too much of it.

5.

May she not know an adder in her breast,
May she not host a demon as her guest,

May she not find an union in her glass,
May she not marry a good natured ass,
 - Do I mean that? no, let her learn that "mine"
In the language of mortals is
Dubious currency, a tricky decibel,
Still, not to be sniffed at if she's a woman
At all: she may not be the worse for human love.
I find this letter Paul hard to end:
The skein of madness tends to unravel
Into boleros Ravel never dreamed of:
But from my chambers in James's Street
I am yours, Man, Woman, Child, Trinity.

Dublin 1969

HEIMWEH

To have *Heimweh* for a madhouse
To half-hear Jaime when he discusses Sender
(Chiefly *cosas amorosas y sexuales*)
To in short be a member of an institution
For medicated vegetables, is not a solid preparation
For the infrequent 16A and the price of vegetables,
I mean vegetables for real, the moulting cauliflower,
The lecherous carrot, the hearted cabbage,
The mosquish onion, the shrewish radish,
All the bounty men dig in plots,
Not excluding the unchaste celery,
And the parsnip made famous by Yeats,
Whose *Heimweh* for Inisfree is pretty suspect.
But then one suspects them all,
Du Bellay, Donncha Rua, whoever
Was responsible for "Galway Bay" frightening
Manannán on the way to Liverpool,
Dread accompaniment to puke and puddle,
The heart of exile stinking of stale stout:
Porter had a Synge to it but not bottled
Inclement stout that loosens liver and lights.
Ah the relief of Liverpool and the great clock tower.
There are thousands and thousands who've had *Heimweh*
    for Liverpool
But to have it for a madhouse is at least invidious,
To love fiercely the faces of the violently unhappy,
Rhoda the hippopotamus whose daughter's a bitch,
Young snapper who's handy at his wrists,
Minds with just that one mote in them,
The thread that coarsens the turnip:
Such love is certifiable, the lover a fink,
A mind pickled with Gaelic salads,
Unchristian sauces, unfree libations
Fit for Romany, Lascar, Pink,
But surely not for one whose hand
Has cracked the ice in the Holy Water stoup,
Who has stooped and crackled muscles
Before the Ark of the Most High;
But, saving thought: whatever of Him was man
Decidedly was finkish; our iconologists
Depict him long-haired, he lay about

97

Not only in the Garden, went in for love-feasts,
Suffered the ministrations of tarts. His Father
Put him through most drastic therapy:
At a time like that, resurrectionary thoughts were not,
    I'd say, a balsam.

So in all, perhaps He would countenance
Heimweh for a madhouse, humanly speaking
Prefer Rhoda the hippopotamus whose daughter's a bitch,
jack-o'-the-Blade who is handy at his wrists,
And something tells me all those motes,
Collective maculae, might make a beam
That would sustain a sane world, my masters,
And utilise Spandau for peevish purposes.

Who'd be sent there, and by whom, is matter for another poem.

Dublin 1969

ABBEY PRESS LUNCH 3/9/69
for Phil O'Kelly

Airy from early communion with Austin's monks,
Liberty Hall around the corner, I twiddle
Glass of lemony non-sin, dare not fiddle
Proscript of Antrim doctor, forbidden
Alcohol. I talk to Eamon.
Keen on priorities, he dared a Minister,
Daemon-struck, was suspended, let back in.
Long ago for a Larkin under Toto
We mummed together at Olympia.
Now we burble about ancients and Sophocles
In the Kingdom: Mac, great auk in wild earth.
I talk to Alan: not to-day nor yesterday
We had pillow-talk with Hilton:
"Two angels at my bedside!"
Low at High Table, far from Everest's brother,
I am astonished to re-call I
Lugged Laffan across *The Shadowy Waters*: he
Tells of Patrick-Tarry, Scotched in the stalls
Approached by Earnán: "Do you remember me?"
"Indeed I do". Blith on a hustings
Corner-boys cornered him. "Three boos
For Blythe who never blessed himself".
I looked down the table: Senior Critics
Serenade Hunt. But where is Gaby?
Has Fallon fallen by the wayside?
And Ó Faracháin. Has he foreseen
Fion that without doubt is not *Gan Mhoirt*?
(At least my sip). I am happy.
Why do critics bore me, academics awe me
Editors chill me, alone poets and mummers
Throw up a Maginot Front (and we all know what came of that)
Against our common humanity, Huns, Vandals, all
Bent on spoliating the rose,
Redesigning the heart, converting
Tender feelings to colly-wobbles.
And of course even among the poets and mummers
There are Eichmanns and Quislings and types
Who'd be quite happy to be Ministers of Hate,
Or speculate with non-conservationists,
Or curse our beloved clergy,

99

Or even take a turn at harassing Hilary Boyle
- But meandering mind damned
By something said by Vincent D.
I navigate the table and feel fond
Of Finegan, Seamus, Gus and Rushe,
Hunt's starry fays who cluster round their allocated prey
And do their job while I play with mummers.
In conclusion, Phil, while thanking you for lunch,
I've a strong hunch some of the mummers I name-drop
Will come to my funeral. Indeed
You're welcome yourself if you get a comp.
After this mild romp, outside again
To my wonderful city, and the Liffey
Seems to smell of grease-paint,
And clouds are balls of cleansing tissue
And the buses are a toccatta of Galuppi
And lamp-posts reach to the dressing-room
Of stars that, piteously, will survive my poor frail mummers.

POSTCRIPT TO PATRICIAN STATIONS
for Richard Riordan

No more
Like a rat in a corner
No more
Like a bat in a trap
But luminous, humble, triumphant
I accept defeat. I know body and soul
At the feast of trencher-men, trust to the last
In honour, the solemn word, the judicious nod,
O what a sell if body and soul have gone to Pilates.
No matter.   I am still
No more
Like a rat in a corner.

Dublin 1969

CONTRA NATURAM

1.

I am hopeless about
Trees, shrubs, flowers:
Though I suppose
I'd parley with a dandelion or daisy
If my nose were trained
To flair nature:
A rose at a pinch.

In the main
I detest God's very own country
Wild, seed-packeted or parterred.
In my secret walks
I gibber like a loon
Against the Maker:
The wizard of waterfalls
The custodian of cataracts
The majordomo of mountains
The inventor of oaks
The generalissimo of the garden-pea.
And that goes too for
Luna clustered round with all
Her starry what d'ya callums,
Bee-loud glades, airy glens,
The Seven Bens, Everest, Etna:
All "tourist attractions"
Designed to distract from the main issue:
Our insensate daptivity
Our banishment from Eden.

2.

Confession, self-analysis,
Vanity of vanities.
The air this morning
Was veined with ice.
The sky this morning
Had taken the blue-bag.
The light this morning

Was braying like a Sitwell.
I sloshed through a goulasch,
Wet brown leafage.
A brat of a dog
Leaped at me.
The beast was friendly.
A brace of copper beeches
Easy to recognise, and he
Might win me round.

Dublin 1970

SECOND THOUGHTS

Ascending descending
in the ethereal verbena
swallows dip wings
to jazzed-up *paseo*
light, light guerdon
kisses o kisses peach
the stone ochre stone
of the Church of San Pedro.
In the Holy City of Avila.

Coruscating syncopating
ebonite blackness
factitious stars emerald
ruby grenadine
mantillas in apple
waterfalls in silver
pluming smoke palm-trees
odour of cordite.
In the Holy City of Avila.

O what a squall
sent the Sierra
chair hooked table
glass ticked off bottle
little ones ululated
old ones castigated
flight of the innocents
denser the plumage of
"The Eagle of Gredos"
In the Holy City of Avila.

And I curse the turgid
Rene Füllop-Miller
easier not to know
plundered New World gold
paid the last builders' bills
for the Convent of San José.
Did Teresa ever give a damn
for the discalced Indian?
In the Holy City of Avila.

Avila, July 1971

103

WHO WALKS THROUGH SALAMANCA
for Pearse Hutchinson

Who walks through Salamanca
in air of bronze weightless,
forgotten, no, absolved,
the long chains of anguish
slush of three o'clock
in the etiolated mornings
merited pangs
inflicted by the meritless
exploded gladioli
diamonds cutting the panes of the heart.

Who walks through Salamanca
by platinum dreams bespangled,
apprehended, no, encompassed,
the staccati of turpitude
chill of three o'clock
in the horn-torn mornings
gratuitous goring
bulldazed by the goggled
strumpeted lilies
excremental squatting of the soul.

Who dreams in Salamanca
of the flowering body
and the fecund mind
and forgets the rest of Juvenal
the faggotry the screeching
the insatiable women,
phoenixed in bland acceptance
of "the tragic sense of life".
Send us Unamuno both
children of Janus
your aureoled peppery benedictions.

Salamanca, August 1971

FACILITY
for Paul Durcan

O Carla little girl
in red or checkered apron
you crossed the gravel paths

You did not bring innocence
tokens only of morning
which affright the rest of the day

By now young woman
you have crossed the quarry
and hold yourself at bay

Little Carla
you are remembered
in this poem

Dublin, January 22nd, 1973

ON FIRST HEARING OF THE DEATH OF W.H.AUDEN

Peech, tangerine,
The clouds, the mortals,
And the bus
Toward Ròdos.

All the glitter of cats
Ignorant of passing
Departing shrouds.

The mewling icons are playing *veroñicas*
The prepuced minarets are weeping
And the conserved hinds and does
And all manner of things
Shed ironic mourning.

So do the copper-haired Graces,
The single *Suzuki* decked with carnations,
The nits in the public places
And my sprig of caraway from the mosque.

Layabout strangers
Limestone specialists
Lingering serenaders
Lament an exodus

Myrtles are not in fashion.
I am tormented by ignorance of the names of flowers.
I pick up my match-box.
I read, "Wistaria".
"Wistaria", Wystan, wanhope, Wien.

Limestone into limestone.

Ròdos, 2-3 October 1973

A NOTE TO MY AUNTIE

The children knew even the eggs' colours,
could recognize a kind of mushroom,
might even at a pinch recognize,
nay, dear Auntie, consider the quality in trees.

You know I had a gap in my youth,
Great Masters took the mickey out of me.
Those who rot in cities
ought, should they not, have lived
in arboured, floral, turdy culture,
our country cousins in the plashy
fields of crozierdom.

Dear Auntie, was this Original Sin?

Dublin 1973

AFTER THE "SENTENCES" OF A.C. (1896 - 1974)

They talk of peace with justice
Parade their rosary ways
But we remember how they tortured
Stephen Hayes.

Dublin 28 December 1974

107

PASTICHE

"Thomas McGreevy
Heard unearthly music
Passing westward
Over Stephen's Green"

When was that written?
What year of the salads?
With whom did I share the crystal?
How long after the poor bitch Europe
Ceased to quiver?

I think it was forty-eight
A year of premature resurrection
A year of dung and primroses;
The man in Portugal will tell you.

But we all forget so much:
Crystal, primroses, dung.
That man who announced his parity of spirit,
His intention to read all Shaw,
Then ascend into Heaven.
The patience of Job cannot make us Marcels.

The unearthly music has passed by.

Dublin, 19-20 February 1975

A PAELLA FOR DRIVELLERS

"And *Swift* expires a *Driv'ler* and a *Show*".
Samuel Johnson: *The Vanity of Human Wishes*

1.

Translated from Mater of Misericordia
To Pater of *saeva indignatio*
(That way the classical finks like Bobbie Graves
Can't get at you: though I could
Beat most of them at their olives and *ludus*)
Is best perhaps a time to take stocks:
Verbena annoys me: what does it smell like?
Also the gladioli the two Marys brought me
And were flushed by some prunish sister
Or some old segotia over-doing his duty.
(In Mercer's a dear old thing
Grieved the absence of brandies
And nice things on the Christmas board,
She'd had a Guinness or two, God help her.)

"Beauty is difficult", Yeats told the
Pigeon and Pound quoted him from
His Pisan cage. The old muddled
Eagle snarled at Paquin. O what
An imprisonment was his: not even
Old Graves could let his portrait
Rest in peace in the White House in Limerick.
Ugliness is difficult. Claudius Graves
Achieved it. My curse on the sage.
May his translations from Suetonius to Apuleius
Prove inaccurate: his novels be
Pulped for faeces-paper:
The Tonton Macoute be his Legio Mariae:
His White Goddess be proven a personal deity of Perón:
His fame be enshrined in the theology of Father O'Flynn
Or Maeterlinck the guest of Salazar.
Let him be honoured by the Caudillo,
Haunted by the shades of Allende and Neruda

May the shade of La Passionaria
Vomit the blood of the innocent
On his perfidious Anglo-Irish ashes:
Albion's paltry gain is Ireland's
Unspeakably sales-bargain loss. We
Salute Tom Moore, the friend of
Emmet and Byron: he never
Sold his soul for a pottage
Of peevery against giants.
Bobbie's last ride with Laura made him no Petrarch.
I hate him. Hatred is good
When it is for the senile monomaniac,
For the lowest type of Irishman,
The begrudger. Yes, he is a good poet.
P.G.Wodehouse was a good jester.
William Joyce was a good newscaster.
They had not the time to strip
Yeats and Joyce and Eliot and
Poor great Ezra whose Cantos are
Our glory, our blotched marvellous glory.
Our Europe, mullioned, impounded
In choate tiles of splendour.

2.

But I wander as usual.
I could never be Leander.
For my heroes are people I fear to fight for.
Jews, Sephardic and Ashkenazy,
Palestine refugees, disloyal Kurds,
The world's great galaxy of Nansens,
God's chosen miserable. The
Most I would or might do would
Be defend a queer or take
Umbrage against nigger-haters.

110

O Lord why are we so afraid.
We should not need miracles.
Moses and Aaron did their thing in their time.
So did Jesus. But they were
Superstars setting precedents which
Were not guaranteed for eternal charts:
Planets have been violated (I
Suppose of course Jesus violated Earth)
And yet we are afraid of things
Less mundane than miracles:
Afraid of our neighbours' good will,
Afraid of our enemies' plámás,
Afraid of our priests, our public servants,
Afraid of the Jones's car,
Afraid of ourselves and the Unknown Gods
While Saintly Bobbie lives,
Scandalizes the good people of Limerick,
For which he professed himself homesick.

4.

Yes: Eavan Boland, poet and daughter of Elizabeth's Chancellor,
Was right. I am mentally sick:
Sick of verbena and gladioli and Graves.
My place is St. Elizabeth's.
Not this Swiftian haven where even the mad are human
And the Unknown God turds a globule of grace.
Lord I am grateful even for being afraid,
And I remember you Faith Burton
Who thought you were a tram,
And you dear Covington who were bled by faggotry, Gésinus
        and leukemia,
And Anton of the grimed ivory neck,
Mason who Candied up with Terry,
Whisky in Vaucresson, Pernod
When the movie-director's wife,
Stuffed with baby, stuffed me with
Francs in the Bar Vert.

Above all, Lord, Unknown God,
I am grateful for finding
My choate tiles of splendour
In poor human beasts,
Not in *putti* or medalions.
These human things are all we have.
God, Unknown or *à la* Nine Fridays
Be good to them. God bless *le moineau*
And make her a good girl.
Rich and rare were the gems she wore.
Now we are rid of our greatest carbuncle.

Austin, though you are cinders,
Thou should'st be with us now.

STAFF NURSE

She is above bed-pans.
The bawls of trapped buttocks
For attention do not move her.
If in eternity of alluminium vice
Muscle shifted and hope was lost
In the bed of excrement,
The ice of her scorn
Would frigidare the Bold Fenian Men,
For she is cold as the Hell of the Gael.

She never heard a nightingale,
Might fancy herself as Cavell at dawn;
Yet would put the fear of God
In that Albanian nun who rescues little ones
From garbage; in my dreams
She is Irma the Terrible.
O lady, you are harsh,
I pray you be not harsher when
Raised to the Sisterhood.

Dublin 1976

POOR ANNA

Poor Anna Wickham
Hung herself on Haverstock.
As the noose released
The giant Antipodean frame
Did the embering anima
Trapeze the juniper years
Paris at dawn and the gendarme
Finding her Pisan in an archway?
Vous êtes Americaine, says he.
Je suis poète, says she.

Poor Anna Wickham
Hung herself on Haverstock.
Lesbos, burning Sappho,
And the tonic sea.

Dublin 1976

DURING THE ILLNESS OF DOLORES IBARRURI

The honourable old woman returns
Treasured by all: even brown.
The forty years have been worth it,
But the cracked heart knows its frown.

Not alone Spain's spirit
But of all who care
For dignity, love, comradeship,
For minutes night rare.

And I think of Kathleen Daly Clarke
Whom we exported to English welfare,
And her spouse the tobacconist.

Madrid 6, 7, 8 September 1977

UNTITLED

"Before the Revolution Spain was a glory".

It has not nor had ever ceased such
For those who dangerously, cruelly
Have loved her.
The packaged tourist may
Wish it otherwise,
The brash young English well-bred
With the shameful thighs
And colonial pigmentation,
May think the dagos nice
But hard to grasp.

"After the Revolution Spain is a glory".

It has not nor had ever ceased such.

MARIPOSAS: SPAIN 1977

All the butterflies of the world
Flutter over your tawniness.
Red, naturally, even yellow
Black and blue tends to shadow
Its desperate maculae
But still salutes.

If only my banana green
Could brush your
Costly fragility.
There would be an encounter.

FOR JULIUS HENRY MARX (1891 - 1977)

Among the blazing azaleas
Of the Parque del Campo Grande
I perceived the true, sophisticated
Marxist point of view:
Let the people have duck soup;
Let them at the races lose their shirts,
let them shirtless storm the Opera,
And stop the shrieks of Mimi with Coronas.
Chiefly, let them raise intemperate eyebrows
To the infinite spaces of the stars.

Valladolid-Madrid, August/September 1977

116

TO Ms MAE WEST ON HER 85th

What right have you?
Did you pat your platinum alps
When across the electric wire
The thrilling message came
That the pelvic muscles were tranquillized
The gluteal shivers forever fridged
That in fact (O lamentable extinction!)
Elvis had gone pop?

Or did you cable another Cadillac
To some lucky mother-doll of Christ's
Or over caskets run your pensive eye,
Golden, placid, lined with peachy silk,
And have your Self remeasured
For the last tango with the beautician
Who'll set all curves in proper mould,
The plastic dugs on top?

I weep not for the King: he wasn't my type.
(Well, give him some pink, false roses.)
But you, old timer, had better go West
While the pickings (pan me a nugget, Beulah)
Are ripe. The blue jeans of yesteryear
Might yet reverence your mummy,
And e'en their grassed spawn be mesmerized.

Vallodolid, 17 August, 1977

117

WITHOUT HER CLOAK

The last time we met
(Mild May before the year you plunged
                    into strong waters)
You said, "They were very good to me".
So in walled Avila of unspeakable Teresa
I recalled you to the manager of the Hotel Jardín.
It was the Feast of the Assumption.

A useful cliché that same high Castilian courtesy.
Fortuitously of course the argent is real.
When I told him you were dead
    (Dead, though you walk beside me,
    cloaked, ribald, vulnerable)
His dark mild eyes crinkled.
The argent real was in his threnody:
La pobre Mees Katie - twice.

Vallodolid, August 1977

PIEDAD

I am lame at the bar in Atocha.
"Your knee is wounded" she says.
I press a coin in her copper palm.
She gives me a prayer for graces
From the Christ: composed by a foreigner,
Gemma Galgani.
Lord, am I in eternal Spain
Or Italianate Ireland of the craven hussies.

Vallodolid, 21 August 1977

118

SMITH Y JONES

Ben Murphy posa, por dinero desnudo:
Es porque hombre Pete Duell se suicidio?

Bar O'Lar, Vallodolid, 22 August 1977

THE LAST ROMANTIC

I see with love the turbaned skull
The flower hand beckoning to bosky doom.
I see with love the purblind balls
Tracing *Madame Bovary* in an ill-lit room.

Madrid, September 1977

PATRICK (1904 - 1967)

On a Malaga street I saw the spit
Of P.K.: remembered how Patrick
Vaunted his Western ancestry.
I wonder now if perhaps
The King of Spain's daughter
Had a dug in it?

P.K.

A quiet spot in peaceful Inniskeen
Seems bleak enough in a mid-winter scene.

But warmer far than mundane minds can know
This near celestial force dispels the snow.

To those who thrill his wondrous lines to read,
He is not dead but much alive indeed.

MICHEÁL
25 October 1899 - 6 March 1978

Doffed the curious toupées
Unflaked the valorous *maquillage*
— A pale olive haze
On special days
As when Lennox
Going to the Ball
Plastered his face green
For no reason at all
The great player relaxes
(Does he smoke a Celtique?)
Waits for this ultimate call.
"O what will people say?"

In a sub-tropical garden
Drenched in moonlight
Moths, midges, white butterflies,
Die on my cheeks
As I cry for you.

Málaga, August 1978

MÁLAGA

'*Es un loco?*'" - was my roar,
When the nutty Andaluz awoke me,
Prodded, scratched, sibilant for cigarettes.
'*Un poco mas o menos*', yawned the whore.
'A little more or less.'
And then no more while the tawny beast
From the heavens consumed me.

That night the monkey
Peddled me grass from the port,
Fresh weed of Africa
But I cast my bread on coarse gin,
Slugged in the ebony and spume of dawn.

Málaga, August 1978

FLYING MEN

"Come fly to me"
Was his Master's voice
And Joseph of Copertino zoomed.
Come fly with me"
Was his own hortation
And he seized the Confessor of
The Convent of Fossombrone,
Took him, men, on a trip.

But O the Chevalier Baldassare
Who had fierce O such fierce tremors!
At Assisi they say it happened.
Joseph grabbed him by the hair
Wheeled him round in aether
And from the brightness of the air
Set him down safe O untrembling.

We Irish are not to be undone.
We have our very own flying man.
No monk I grant you, but almost as good,
He was cursed by one.

His name was Suibhne.

Dublin, May 25, 1979

123

THE POETIC TOUCH

A dachshund races a lawn-mower.
There are John West salmon roses
And cream. A deserted plastic swan
Keels in the parched grass. These things,
I reckon, our rostrum explicators
Would bid us dwell upon.

I cannot make it new.
Light glints in crevices of cloud:
Enough to be doing with.

Churchtown, June 1979

LOLEK

Czestochowa, Jasna Gora,
        Auschwitz, Nova Huta:
Archdiocesan Cracow:

Symphony of ashed flesh and steel and Mary,
Uncountable dark nights in the factory of death,
Salvos of laud on the Black Virgin's White Mountain,
The people of God keen from metal with metamorphosed hearts
Expectancy and rose of Christ's fair state
You have known it all:
Grease-paint, desk, sledge-hammer,
Arc-light, explosive, grammar,
Mickiewicz's mighty line,
More resounding than Wagnerian microphones,
Juliusz Slowacki in the Szkackas' drawingroom,
Promethean Cyprian Norwid,
Poor Zegladlowicz who pained the clergy
And Juan de la Cruz wrestling,
Parched in a tawny landscape,
With the Angel of Faith.

You expect much faith from Patrick's children.
In this our pleasant land of Country and Western singers,
So great a hope as yours must find it.
And meantime - while the phones ring
        and the keys tap and the words spawn -
Let the chisellers and the unstained
Sing a carol for Karol:
"May Holy Ireland be holier,
Perhaps even made whole".

Feast of the Assumption, Dublin 1979

ST. PIUS WARD
for Brendan Harding

Stately, scrawny, hot-eyed, head alert
To some unearthly music, and O steered
By twin snowy handmaidens, he proceeds
In majesty: plucking at some
Kind of embroidery frame, flexed
Frightfully to a flask of bluey wine.

I dread his return. Apocalypse! Cover
Mine eyes. His face dazzles. I live again
The blood-gush of a Catalan Christmas,
Root at the walnuts of a Cardinal's brain.

Christ, that my death were in my arms!

Galway, August 1982

PEACOCK AND LITTLE BULL
for Helen and Ursula

From Doohat to Annaghmakerrig
I slosh through cafe-au-lait pools
Squelch through burns amber leafage
Slag branches where the wind misrules
And cogitate that uncommon fowl
Laid up for how long, O Juno?

How long may that delirium of jewels
Share darkness with rats, straw, calf?
How long will that pomp, that plenitude
Sustain lustre, glitter, sheen,
Against reversion to the brighter scene?

Our peacock no doubt mocks our alien ruth
Perceives for fantasy our callow truth:
His ivory tower that manacled shed
His constant worshipper that small bull's head.

THE SHORT UNHAPPY EXILE OF DON GERALDO
14 May - 21 June 1984

*(para mi amigo, John Liddy, gran
aficionado de las cantinas, como yo)*

I wished to die, but yes, I wished to die,
till they said I'd drive them mad,
but not in a clean and well-lit place,
exiled from my things,
from my black tobacco,
from my roses,
from the street
Garlos Gross had them name for me,
poor Carlos whom I've survived.

Quiero morirme
here in Alhaurin el Grande
babbling they'd have me believe
of my dear glamorous shades,
of Lytton and Ralph and Carrington,
of Leonard, Virginia and Morgan,
Yes, I wish to die.

Only let me connect,
dreaming, dreaming, dreaming,
till they raise the coverlet
beyond my nostrils.

TWO YEARS AGO
for Dermot Healy

And Pearse Hutchinson opined
That in *The Sunday Times*
Cocteau looked like Will Hay.

And Brian Coffey silvered
When informed that Patrick K.
Had a strong line in Marian tocsins.

And John O'Connor in Leningrad
Was too shy to tangle
With bardic Irish firemen.

And beyond the magniloquent frost
I wish I remembered more
Than a couple of fountains,
Some dishevelled roses,
Some errant swallows
And my heart like a braying ass.

28 February 1988

LITIR DO CHAILÍN NÁR CHASADH ORM ARIAMH

Ní liomthach mé i do theangain
ach creidim go bhfuil teanga idirnáisúnta an chroí
ar fáil do gach duine.
Trachtáil mí-shuaimhneach ag tarraingt
                           go teann im fhíor-anam
is tusa led chroiceann mhín
is led thréan - duilleog gruaige
ag fanúint ar crannaibh silíní.

Is mise im aonar
táid uile dearmhadta agam
Helen Kide is Bertha Big-Foot
is buachaillí m'uilc
is béal scáth mo mhaithre
gan do chroiceann agamsa
gan duilleog
is níl cúis agam Chrith ag fanúint
ar crannaibh silíní.

GA

Ós rud é gurbh daonna é
Do tharraing an ga na chléibh
Aithne níos cruinne ná sna bhlianta spailpín dó
Ar aighthe na h-úrnaighe
Ar an útamáil ar an bpotaireacht
Ar theangmháil an chré ar a chneis
Ar cumhracht alluis a mhuintir
Bfhéidir gur shil grá leis an gcorcra
Don chrainn fhíge do mhaslaigh sé

THE HERO

(Translated from the Irish, "An Laoch",
of Micheál Mac Liammóir)

The sky on fire
the water a mirror of blood
the mountain threatening
the wind silent
and the waves
splashing
against a sea-weeded
harbour that's been forgotten
long ago.
   Now the sun is going down
   the last mower leaving
   field and meadow
   even
   the curlew
   has gone to sleep
Now there are only
stoes wild flowers
barefooted children:
children playing making sport
among themselves
on the hillside:
and the memory of a man
who used dream of death
since the rocks
the wild flowers
the barefooted children
were too beautiful too lonely
for him to be able to go on
living in their midst.
   Look now:
   The flowers are withered
   the children are
   but ghosts
   here there are only stones
   and blackness of the night
   above them

Ros Muc, 1951

LITTLE SECRET DESIRES

(Translated from the Irish, "Na Mionmhianta
Faoi Rún" of Micheál Mac Liammóir)

And will I ever see again
the rose springing in the mountain-snow
the star glittering in the well-bottom
the woman dancing in the burning house?

Or the butterfly blue within the Cathedral
the man naked in St. Stephen's Green
the winged angel in the prison courtyard
the grinning cat on the judge's bench.

UNTITLED

Sur le bord de la flaque un oiseau s'est posé
Mais il n'a pas chanté
Pourquoi alors s'est-il posé?

Pour regarder les nuages passer
Glisser du gris sans bruit
Dans l'eau grise d'une flaque

Ou boire l'eau délaissée
Par le ciel de la nuit
Sur le bord de la flaque un oiseau s'est posé

Dans le vent et les branches baissées
Il a vu se rider la marque
De ses plumes où l'ombre s'est penchée

Lors les belles couleurs nées du vent
S'égaraient à ses plumes
Les belles couleurs qui font des ronds sous les yeux clos

Des pages de nuages gondolées par les ondes
Passaient entre les ondes
Nuages ou vieux papiers d'une boîte de chocolats

La flaque était un lac au creux d'une pierre-ponce
Sur la rive mouille une ombre toujours là
Crevée en un buisson ardent

Crevée par l'angle oblique de l'iris
Or - curieusement tout fonce
Et l'eau devient trop lisse

Penché il allait transpercer le papier des nuages
L'oiseau allait ouvrir l'image
Et retrouver le ciel profond au fond de l'eau

Il a un bec au milieu de ses plumes irisées
Il a un bec corné
Affreux et mort comme un ongle de pied

Son bec dur et vorace a rayé le miroir
Son bec sans douceur est une sangsue noire
Collée à la silhouette qui se redresse pour boire

Faites-lui peur - qu'il s'envole - je ne veux plus le voir...

NOTES

First Letter: to Donal O'Farrell;   a friend from the author's schooldays at Synge Street.

Pub Poem of the '40s; "Conveyed by the Bishop of Nara" - titular bishopric of the Archdiocese of Dublin.

Ode to Michael Gill, ESQ; first published in The National Student, December 1949, under the pseudonym Mr Jenkins. Michael Gill is the publisher whose company later became Gill and Macmillan.

Wordsworth Was Right; the "he" and the "Patrick" refer to Patrick Kavanagh, a friend of John Jordan's.

Second Letter: to Patrick Swift; Patrick Swift, (1928-1983), artist and writer, a friend from the author's schooldays; editor of the literary magazine "X". Settled in the Algarve in the 1960s. With David Wright he wrote three books on Portuguese Regions.

Eclectic; this is the original draft of a poem which in February 1975 the author re-worked and published under the title "Pastiche" in "With Whom Did I Share the Crystal?"

A Dialogue; Justin Keating: former Labour Party politician, son of the painter Sean Keating (1889-1977)

Fourth Letter: to David Posner; a friend of the author from his postgraduate days at Pembroke College, Oxford.

"Entre Chat et Loup"; "entre chien et loup" - in the dusk of evening; Quentin Stevenson, English poet born 1935, the author's colleague at Oxford University, 1954-55. Joint editor of the Oxford literary magazine "Trio". His early poems were concerned with religious themes.

Self Portrait: Oxford; published as the first of two verses entitled "Two Self-Sketches", in "With Whom Did I Share the Crystal?"

Elegiac Notes on R.C.; originally published in Arena, issue 1, under the pen-name Stephen Renehan. R.C., Robert Bolquhoun, the Scots painter, graduate of the Glasgow School of Art; member of the Soho set of Freud and Bacon; companion of Robert MacBryde.

One Who was not Invited; Telefís Éireann is the official title of the Irish Television Service; l.14, Fianna Fail and Fine Gael are the Republic's chief political parties; l.20, Mr Michael Scott was the donor of the Tower; l.22, Mrs Dolly Robinson was the first Curator of the Tower; l.25, Con is the familiar appelation of both Dr. A.J.Leventhal and the late Dr. C.P.Curran.

Tidings from Breda; "Joaquin", a young man from Galicia. "Maria Antonia", Sra Puig-Bo de Piera; "Free Cubas", Cuba libre. Spanish for rum-and-coke. "Prici" a Barcelona eating-house; "Nati" a Barcelona landlady; "Toni and Mati" Sr and Sra Toni Turull. "Harden" Mrs Harden Rodgers Jay. "Leland", Mrs Leland Bardwell. "John" Mr John Jay. "Con" Dr A.J.Leventhal. "Dickie", Dr Richard Riordan. "Paddy dear" Mr P.J.Clancy; Title of a poem by Mr James Liddy; "Dara" Mr Macdara Woods; "Carrol's Special" Dr Anthony Carroll.

Athens; published as the second of two verses entitled "Two Self-Sketches" in "With Whom Did I Share the Crystal?"

To the People of Libya; King Idris was still in power, occupying quarters of the British base of Beirut.

Imagist Poem in Islam; refers to the author's friend Richard Riordan, poet and medical doctor whom John Jordan visited in Libya.

A Minor Complication; l.22, Liam Ó Briain, born Dublin 1888; took part in the 1916 Rising; interned at Curragh Camp, 1921. Professor of Romance Languages U.C.G., 1917-58. Founder and director of Taibhearc na Gaillimhe.

Feast of St. Justin; Stephen Hayes, IRA leader of the 1940s, who was interrogated by his subordinates and deposed as leader. See author's poem "After the Sentences of A.C."

Letter To Paul; Paul Durcan, born 1944, poet, a student of Mr Jordan at University College, Dublin, and a friend subsequently.

Abbey Press Lunch; Phil O'Kelly, Abbey Theatre manager,

1967-71, resigned when he was not given a seat on the board, 1971.

1,5: Eamon - Eamon Keane, 1925-1990, actor with the Abbey and Gate companies and with the R.T.É. rep.

1,11: "In the Kingdom: Mac". Anew MacMaster, celebrated actor/director, 1894-1962.

1,12: Alan Simpson, 1920-1982, director of several theatres in Dublin.

1,17: Laffan, Patrick Laffan, actor and director of the Peacock Theatre.

142. Hilary Boyle, well-known as a social reformer/crusader in Dublin in the sixties.

1,46: names of theatre critics and journalists.

During the Ilness of Dolores Ibarurri: celebrated defender of the Spanish Republic; known as La Passionaria. Thomas Clarke, 1857-1916, revolutionary, who had a tobacconist's shop at 75a Great Britain St., now Parnell St., Dublin.

Without Her Cloak: Kate O'Brien, novelist, friend of the author.

St. Pius Ward: refers to the author's hospitalisation in Galway, 1n 1982, and is dedicated to a doctor who treated him there.

Litir do Chailín: undated, found among MSS.

GA; undated; original written under the nom de plume Brendan Pleimionn. Published in Broadsheet no 10, March 1970

Untitled: found among Mr Jordan's papers. Quite probably his own composition, given his fluency in French, in which he took a first class honours degree at U.C.D., winning the Laforcade medal in 1951.